Service Design based on ITIL® V3 - A Man

CW00401568

.

Other publications by Van Haren Publishing

Van Haren Publishing (VHP) specializes in titles on Best Practices, methods and standards within IT management, Architecture (Enterprise and IT), business management and project management.

These publications are grouped in series, eg: *ITSM Library* (on behalf of ITSMF International), *Best Practice* and *IT Management Topics*. VHP is also publisher on behalf of leading companies and institutions, eg The Open Group, IPMA-NL, CA, Getronics, Pink Elephant. At the time of going to press the following books are available:

IT (Service) Management / IT Governance
ITSM, ITIL® V3 and ITIL® V2
Foundations of IT Service Management – based on ITIL® V3 (English, Dutch, German; French, Japanese and Spanish editions)
Introduction to IT Service Management (ITIL V3, English)
IT Service Management based on ITIL V3 – A Pocket Guide (English, Dutch, German, Italian; French, Japanese and Spanish editions)
Foundations of IT Service Management based on ITIL® (ITIL V2), (English, Dutch, French, German, Spanish, Japanese, Chinese, Danish, Italian, Korean, Russian, Arabic)
Implementing Service and Support Management Processes (English)
Release and Control for IT Service Management, based on ITIL® – A Practitioner Guide (English)

ISO/IEC 20000
ISO/IEC 20000 – An Introduction (English, German)
Implementing ISO/IEC 20000 Certification (English)
ISO/IEC 20000 – A Pocket Guide (English, Italian, German, Spanish, Portuguese)

ISO 27001 and ISO 17799
Information Security based on ISO 27001 and ISO 17799 – A Management Guide (English)
Implementing Information Security based on ISO 27001 and ISO 17799 – A Management Guide (English)

COBIT
IT Governance based on COBIT4.1® – A Management Guide (English, German, Japanese)

IT Service CMM
IT Service CMM – A Pocket Guide (English)

ASL and BiSL
ASL – A Framework for Application Management (English, German)
ASL – Application Services Library – A Management Guide (English, Dutch)
BiSL – A Framework for Business Information Management (Dutch, English)
BiSL – Business information Services Library – A Management Guide (Dutch; English)

ISPL
IT Services Procurement op basis van ISPL (Dutch)
IT Services Procurement based on ISPL – A Pocket Guide (English)

Other IT Management titles:
De RfP voor IT-outsourcing (Dutch; English version due Spring 2008)
Decision- en Controlfactoren voor IT-Sourcing (Dutch)
Defining IT Success through the Service Catalogue (English)
Frameworks for IT Management – An introduction (English, Japanese; German)
Frameworks for IT Management – A Pocket Guide (English, German, Dutch)
Implementing IT Governance (English)
Implementing leading standards for IT management (English, Dutch)
IT Service Management global best practices, volume 1 (English)
IT Service Management Best Practices, volume 1, 2, 3 and 4 (Dutch)
ITSM from hell! / ITSM from hell based on Not ITIL (English)
ITSMP – The IT Strategy Management Process (English)

Metrics for IT Service Management (English, Russian)
Service Management Process Maps (English)
Six Sigma for IT Management (English)
Six Sigma for IT Management – A Pocket Guide (English)

MOF/MSF
MOF – Microsoft Operations Framework, A Pocket Guide (Dutch, English, French, German, Japanese)
MSF – Microsoft Solutions Framework, A Pocket Guide (English, German)

Architecture (Enterprise and IT)
TOGAF, The Open Group Architecture Framework – A Management Guide (English)
The Open Group Architecture Framework – 2007 Edition (English, official publication of TOG)
TOGAF™ Version 8 Enterprise Edition – Study Guide (English, official publication of TOG)
TOGAF™ Version 8.1.1 Enterprise Edition –A Pocket Guide (English, official publication of TOG)

Business Management
ISO 9000
ISO 9001:2000 – The Quality Management Process (English)

EFQM
The EFQM excellence model for Assessing Organizational Performance – A Management Guide (English)

SqEME®
Process management based on SqEME® (English)
SqEME® – A Pocket Guide (English, Dutch)

Project/Programme/Risk Management
ICB/NCB
NCB Versie 3– Nederlandse Competence Baseline (Dutch, on behalf of IPMA-NL)
Projectmanagement op basis van NCB V3 – IPMA-C en IPMA-D (Dutch)

PRINCE2™
Project Management based on PRINCE2™– Edition 2005 (English, Dutch, German)
PRINCE2™ – A No Nonsense Management Guide (English)
PRINCE2™ voor opdrachtgevers – Management Guide (Dutch)

MINCE®
MINCE® – A Framework for Organizational Maturity (English)

MSP
Programme Management based on MSP (English, Dutch)
Programme Management based on MSP – A Management Guide (English)

M_o_R
Risk Management based on M_o_R – A Management Guide (English)

Other publications on project management:
Wegwijzer voor methoden bij Projectvolwassenheid (Dutch: fall 2008)
Het Project Management Office – Management Guide (Dutch)

For the latest information on VHP publications, visit our website: www.vanharen.net

Service Design
based on ITIL® V3

A Management Guide

Colophon

Title:	Service Design based on ITIL® V3 - A Management Guide
Authors:	Jan van Bon (Chief Editor, Inform-IT) Arjen de Jong (co-author, Inform-IT) Axel Kolthof (co-author, Inform-IT) Mike Pieper (co-author, Inform-IT) Ruby Tjassing (co-author, Inform-IT) Annelies van der Veen (co-author, Inform-IT) Tieneke Verheijen (co-author, Inform-IT)
Copy editor:	Jayne Wilkinson
Publisher:	Van Haren Publishing, Zaltbommel, www.vanharen.net
Design & layout:	CO2 Premedia bv, Amersfoort - NL
ISBN:	9789087531256
Edition:	First edition, first impression, June 2008

Foreword

ITIL receives more and more attention on a global scale, with many companies adopting its principles. In that respect, ITIL version 2 has done a good job. The update of ITIL in version 3, released in June 2007, has caused some concern for many of these companies, since it built on the idea that companies had already achieved results with version 2 content. In practice however, most companies are still working their way through the basic principles of ITIL. For that reason, the "Foundations of IT Service Management - based on ITIL V3" was developed, offering a comprehensive but easy-to-understand source of information on ITIL. This title is now widely used as the authoritative guide on ITIL V3 in training situations and in implementations.

Apart from offering the market a summarized, easy-to-understand source on ITIL V3, that can be used for a step-by-step approach, many companies focus on a subset of the ITIL best practices. That is why we developed a series of ITIL Management Guides, focusing on the processes, procedures, and functions, from each of the phases of the ITIL V3 Lifecycle. This enables companies to focus on those phases that are of primary concern to them.

Each of the five ITIL V3 Management Guides is structured the same way as the successful Foundations book: it separates the Lifecycle information from the single process, procedure and function components, enabling organizations to take their own approach and still adopt ITIL best practices.

The content of each guide was derived from the Foundations book, which ensures that you'll find the same high quality as usual. This means that all content has been peer-reviewed in a rigorous way, making sure that it completely aligns to ITIL V3, but also that it was the best, concise and comprehensive summary of ITIL V3 core content that could be achieved.

I'm convinced that this new management guide will provide an excellent reference tool for practitioners, students and others who want to have a practical guide on the key ITIL V3 concepts.

Jan van Bon
Chief Editor

Acknowledgements

This Management Guide is a compilation of the itSMF publication "Foundations of IT Service Management - Based on ITIL V3". Thus, the international review team that reviewed "Foundations of IT Service Management", has contributed indirectly to this Management Guide. We would like to thank all reviewers once again for their detailed review which improved the quality of both books significantly.

The review team consists of:
- John van Beem, ISES International, Netherlands
- Aad Brinkman, Apreton, Netherlands
- Peter Brooks, PHMB Consulting, itSMF South Africa
- Rob van der Burg, Microsoft, Netherlands
- Judith Cremers, Getronics PinkRoccade Educational Services, Netherlands
- Robert Falkowitz, Concentric Circle Consulting, itSMF Switzerland
- Rosario Fondacaro, Quint Wellington Redwood, Italy
- Peter van Gijn, LogicaCMG, Netherlands
- Jan Heunks, ICT Partners, Netherlands
- Linh Ho, Compuware Corporation, USA
- Ton van der Hoogen, ToTZ Diensten, Netherlands
- Kevin Holland, NHS, UK
- Matiss Horodishtiano, Amdocs, itSMF Israel
- Wim Hoving, BHVB, Netherlands
- Brian Johnson, CA, USA
- Georges Kemmerling, Quint Wellington Redwood, Netherlands
- Kirstie Magowan, itSMF New Zealand
- Steve Mann, OpSys - SM2, itSMF Belgium
- Reiko Morita, Ability InterBusiness Solutions, Inc., Japan
- Jürgen Müller, Marval Benelux, Netherlands
- Ingrid Ouwerkerk, Getronics PinkRoccade Educational Services, Netherlands
- Ton Sleutjes, CapGemini, Netherlands
- Maxime Sottini, Innovative Consulting, itSMF Italy
- Takashi Yagi, Hitachi Ltd., itSMF Japan

Given the desire for a broad consensus in the IT Service Management field, new developments, additional material and contributions from ITSM professionals who have worked with ITIL version 3 are welcome. They will be discussed by the editors and where appropriate incorporated into new editions. Comments can be sent to the Chief Editor, Jan van Bon, email: j.van.bon@inform-it.org.

Contents

X

CHAPTER 1

Introduction

1.1 Background

Developments in IT have had a tremendous effect on the business market during the last decade. Since the appearance of extremely powerful hardware, highly versatile software and super-fast networks, all connected to each other worldwide, organizations have been able to develop their information-dependent products and services to a greater extent, and to bring them to the market much faster. These developments have marked the transition of the industrial age into the **information age**. In the information age, everything has become faster and more dynamic, and everything is connected.

Traditional hierarchical organizations often have difficulties in responding to this rapidly changing market, and this has led to current trends for organizations to become flatter and more flexible. The focus has shifted from vertical silos to horizontal **processes**, and decision-making powers are increasingly bestowed on the employees. It is against this background that the work processes of IT service management have arisen.

An important advantage of process-oriented organizations is that processes can be designed to support a **customer-oriented approach**. This has made the alignment between the IT organization (responsible for supplying information) and the customer (responsible for using these information systems in their business) increasingly significant. Over the last couple of years, this trend has attracted attention under the title of **Business-IT Alignment (BITA)**.

As organizations gained more experience with the **process-oriented approach** of IT service management, it became clear that the process must be managed coherently.

Furthermore, it was obvious that the introduction of a process-oriented work method meant a big change for the primarily line and project-oriented organizations. Culture and change management proved to be crucial elements for a successful organizational design.

Another important lesson learned was that the IT organization must not lose itself in a process culture. Just like the one-sided project-oriented organization, a one-sided process-oriented organization was not the optimum type of business. Balance was, as always, the magic word. In addition, it became clear that the customer-oriented approach required that an **end-to-end** and **user-centric** approach must be followed: it was of no help to the user to know that "the server was still in operation" if the information system was not available at the user's workplace. IT services must be viewed in a larger context. The need for the recognition of the **Service Lifecycle**, and the management of IT services in light of that lifecycle, became a concern.

Due to the fast growing dependency of business upon information, the quality of information services in companies is being increasingly subjected to stricter **internal and external requirements**. The role of **standards** is getting more and more important, and **frameworks** of "best practices" help with the development of a management system to meet these requirements. Organizations that are not in control of their processes, will not be able to realize great results on the level of the Service Lifecycle and the end-to-end-management of those services. Organizations that do not have their internal organization in order, will also not achieve great results. For these reasons, all these aspects are handled alongside each other in the course of this book.

1.2   Why this book

This book offers detailed information for those who are responsible for strategic information issues, as well as for the (much larger) group who are responsible for setting up and executing the delivery of the information systems. This is supported by both the description of the Service Lifecycle, as documented in ITIL version 3, and by the description of the processes that are associated with it. The ITIL core books are very extensive, and can be used for a thorough study of contemporary best practices. This management guide provides the reader with an easy-to-read comprehensive introduction to the broad library of ITIL core books, to support the understanding and the further distribution of ITIL as an industry standard. Once this understanding of the structure of ITIL has been gained, the reader can use the core books for a more detailed understanding and guidance for their daily practice.

1.3   Organizations

Several organizations are involved in the maintenance of ITIL as a description of the "best practice" in the IT service management field.

OGC

Initially ITIL was a product of the CCTA, a UK Government Organization. On 1 April 2001 the CCTA was incorporated into the OGC, which thus became the new owner of ITIL. The aim of the OGC is to help its clients (within the UK Government) with the modernization of their procurement activities and the improvement of their services, by, among other things, making the best possible use of IT: "OGC aims to modernize procurement in government, and deliver substantial value for money improvements". The OGC promotes the use of "best practices" in numerous areas, such as project management, program management, procurement, risk management and IT service management. For this reason the OGC itself has published several series of books (Libraries) which have been written by (international) experts from different companies and organizations.

itSMF

The target group for this publication is anyone who is involved or interested in IT service management. A professional organization, working on the development of the IT service management field, has been created especially for this target group.

In 1991 the Information Technology Service Management Forum (itSMF), originally known as the Information Technology Infrastructure Management Forum (ITIMF), was set up as a UK association. In 1994, a sister-association was established in the Netherlands, following the UK example.

Since then, independent itSMF organizations have been set up in more than forty countries, spread across the globe, and the number of "chapters" continues to grow. All itSMF organizations operate under the umbrella organization, itSMF International (itSMF-I).

itSMF is aimed at the entire professional area of IT service management. It promotes the exchange of information and experiences that IT organizations can use to improve their service provision. itSMF is also involved in the use and quality of the various standards and methods that are important in the field. One of these standards is ITIL. itSMF International has an agreement with OGC and APM Group on the promotion of the use of ITIL.

APM Group
In 2006, OGC contracted the management of ITIL rights, the certification of ITIL exams and accreditation of training organizations to the APM Group (APMG), a commercial organization. APMG defines the certification and accreditation for the ITIL exams, and published the new certification system (see Section 2.1: ITIL exams).

Exam bodies
The Dutch foundation Examen Instituut voor Informatica (EXIN) and the English Information Systems Examination Board (ISEB, part of the BCS: the British Computer Society) cooperated in the development and provision of certification for IT service management. For many years they were the only bodies that provided ITIL exams. With the contracting of APMG by OGC, the responsibility for ITIL exams is now with APMG. To support the world-wide delivery of these ITIL exams, APMG has accredited a number of exam bodies: EXIN, BCS/ISEB, and Loyalist College, Canada.

1.4   Structure of the book
Chapter 2, introduces the Service Lifecycle, in the context of IT service management and IT governance. It discusses principles of organizational maturity, and the benefits and risks of following a service management framework. This chapter ends with the introduction of the Service Lifecycle.

In Chapters 3 the Service Design lifecycle phase is discussed in detail, in a standardized structure.

Chapter 4 provides general information on principles of processes, teams, roles, functions, positions, tools, and other elements of interest.

In chapter 5, the processes and functions of Service Design are described in detail. Each of these processes and functions is described in terms of:
- Introduction
- Activities, methods and techniques
- Interfaces, inputs and outputs
- Metrics and Key Performance Indicators (KPIs)
- Implementation, with Critical Success Factors (CSFs), challenges, risks and traps

The appendices provide useful sources for the reader. A reference list of used sources is provided, as well as the official ITIL Glossary and a list with acronyms. The book ends with an extensive index of relevant terms that will support the reader in finding relevant text elements.

CHAPTER 2

Introduction to the Service Lifecycle

2.1 Introduction to ITIL

In the 1980s the quality of service provided by both internal and external IT companies to UK government departments was of such a level that the CCTA (Central Computer and Telecommunications Agency, now the Office of Government Commerce, OGC) was instructed by the Government to develop a standard approach for an efficient and effective delivery of IT services. This was to be an approach which was independent of the suppliers (whether internal or external). The result of this instruction was the development and publication of the **Information Technology Infrastructure Library™** (ITIL). ITIL is made up of a collection of "best practices" found across the range of IT service providers.

ITIL offers a systematic approach to the delivery of quality of IT services. It gives a detailed description of most of the important processes in an IT organization, and includes checklists for tasks, procedures and responsibilities which can be used as a basis for tailoring to the needs of individual organizations.

At the same time, the broad coverage of ITIL also provides a helpful reference guide for many areas, which can be used to develop new improvement goals for an IT organization, enabling it to grow and mature.

Over the years, ITIL has become much more than a series of useful books about IT service management. The framework for the "best practice" in IT service management is promoted and further developed by advisors, trainers and suppliers of technologies or products. Since the nineties, ITIL represents not only the theoretical framework, but the approach and philosophy shared by the people who work with it in practice.

Being an extended framework of best practices for IT service management itself, the advantages and disadvantages of frameworks in general, described in Section 2.5, are also applicable to ITIL. Of course, ITIL was developed because of the advantages mentioned earlier. Many of the pointers from "best practices" are intended to avoid potential problems, or, should they occur after all, to solve them.

ITIL exams

In 2007 the APM Group launched a new certification scheme for ITIL, based on ITIL version 3. ITIL version 2 will be maintained for a transition period, continuing until the year 2008. **ITIL version 2** has qualifications on three levels:
• **Foundation** Certificate in IT Service Management
• **Practitioner** Certificate in IT Service Management
• **Manager** Certificate in IT Service Management

Until 2000, some 60,000 ITIL certificates had been distributed and by 2006 the number had reached 500,000 certificates .

For **ITIL version 3** a new system of qualifications has been set up. There are four qualification levels:
• Foundation Level
• Intermediate Level (Lifecycle Stream & Capability Stream)
• ITIL Diploma
• Advanced Service Management Professional Diploma

For more information about the ITIL V3 Qualification Scheme, see http://www.itil-officialsite.com/Qualifications/ITILV3QualificationScheme.asp.

2.2 IT governance

With the growing role of information, information systems and IT service management, the management requirements for IT grew as well. These requirements focus on two aspects: the compliance with internal and external policies, laws and regulations, and the provision of added value to the stakeholders of the organization. IT governance is still a very young discipline, with no more than a few acknowledged standards or frameworks available. In contrast, there are many different definitions of IT governance available. A definition that receives a lot of support is the one by Van Grembergen:

> *IT governance* consists of a comprehensive framework of structures, processes and relational mechanisms. Structures involve the existence of responsible functions such as IT executives and accounts, and a diversity of IT Committees. Processes refer to strategic IT decision-making and monitoring. Relational mechanisms include business/IT participation and partnerships, strategic dialogue and shared learning.

There is a clear distinction between governance and management, suggesting that governance enables the creation of a setting in which others can manage their tasks effectively (Sohal & Fitzpatrick). So IT governance and IT management are two separate entities. IT service management can be considered to be part of the IT management domain, which leaves IT governance in the business or information management domain.

Although many frameworks are characterized as "IT Governance frameworks", such as COBIT and even ITIL, most of them are in fact management frameworks. There is at least one standard for IT Governance available: the local Australian standard for Corporate governance of information and communication technology (AS8015-2005).

2.3 Organizational maturity

From the moment **Richard Nolan** introduced his "staged model" for the application of IT in organizations in 1973, many people have used stepwise improvement models. These models were quickly recognized as suitable instruments for quality improvement programs, thereby helping organizations to climb up the maturity ladder.

Dozens of variations on the theme can easily be found, ranging from trades such as software development, acquisition, systems engineering, software testing, website development, data warehousing and security engineering, to help desks and knowledge management. Obviously the *kaizen* principle (improvement works best in smaller steps) was one that appealed to many.

After Nolan's staged model in 1973, the most appealing application of this modeling was found when the Software Engineering Institute (SEI) of Carnegie Mellon University, USA, published its Software Capability Maturity Model (SW-CMM). The CMM was copied and applied in most of the cases mentioned above, making CMM something of a standard in maturity modeling. The CMM was later followed by newer editions, including CMMI (CMM Integration).

Later, these models were applied in quality management models, like the European Foundation for Quality Management (EFQM). Apart from the broad quality management models, there are several other industry accepted practices, such as Six Sigma and Total Quality Management (TQM) which are complementary to ITIL.

The available standards, and frameworks of best practice, offer guidance for organizations in achieving "operational excellence" in IT service management. Depending upon their stage of development, organizations tend to require different kinds of guidance.

Maturity model: CMMI

In the IT industry, the process maturity improvement process is best known in the context of the **Capability Maturity Model Integration (CMMI)**. This process improvement method was developed by the Software Engineering Institute (SEI) of Carnegie Mellon University. CMMI provides both a staged and a continuous model. In the continuous representation, improvement is measured using capability levels. Maturity is measured for a particular process across an organization. In the staged representation, improvement is measured using maturity levels, for a set of processes across an organization.

The capability levels in the **CMMI continuous representation** are:
- **incomplete process** - a process that either is not performed or partially performed
- **performed process** - satisfies the specific goals of the process area
- **managed process** - a performed (capability level 1) process that has the basic infrastructure in place to support the process
- **defined process** - a managed (capability level 2) process that is tailored from the organization's set of standard processes according to the organization's tailoring guidelines, and contributes work products, measures and other process improvement information to the organizational process assets
- **quantitatively Managed process** - a defined (capability level 3) process that is controlled using statistical and other quantitative techniques
- **optimizing process** - a quantitatively managed (capability level 4) process that is improved based on an understanding of the common causes of variation inherent in the process

The **CMMI staged representation** model defines five maturity levels, each a layer in the base for the next phase in the ongoing process improvement, designated by the numbers 1 through 5:
1. **initial** - processes are ad hoc and chaotic
2. **managed** - the projects of the organization have ensured that processes are planned and executed in accordance with policy
3. **defined** - processes are well characterized and understood, and are described in standards, procedures, tools and methods

4. **quantitatively managed** - the organization and projects establish quantitative objectives for quality and process performance, and use them as criteria in managing processes
5. **optimizing** - focuses on continually improving process performance through incremental and innovative process and technological improvements

Many other maturity models were based on these structures, such as the Gartner Maturity Models. Most of these models are focused at capability maturity. Some others, like KPMG's World Class IT Maturity Model, take a different approach.

Standard: ISO/IEC 20000
Developing and maintaining a quality system which complies with the requirements of the ISO 9000 (ISO-9000:2000) series can be considered a tool for the organization to reach and maintain the system-focused (or "managed" in IT Service CMM) level of maturity. These ISO standards emphasize the definition, description and design of processes. For IT service management organizations, a specific ISO standard was produced: the ISO/IEC 20000 (see Figure 2.1).

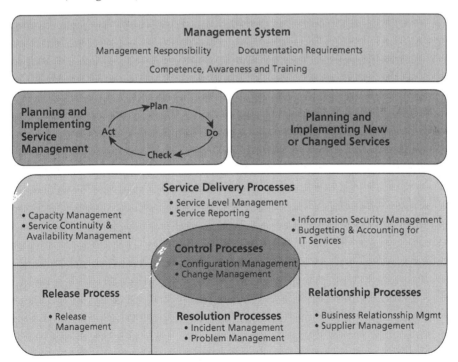

Figure 2.1 Overview of the ISO/IEC 20000 service management system

Customer maturity

When assessing the maturity of an organization, we cannot restrict ourselves to the service provider. The **level of maturity of the customer** (Figure 2.2) is also important. If there are large differences in maturity between the provider and the customer, then these will have to be considered to prevent a mismatch in the approach, methods and mutual expectations. Specifically, this affects the communication between the customer and the provider.

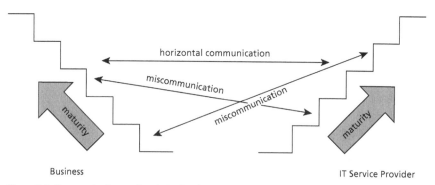

Figure 2.2 Communication and maturity levels: customer and provider

2.4   Benefits and risks of ITSM frameworks

The list below identifies some benefits and possible problems of using IT service management best practices. This list is not intended to be definitive, but is provided here as a basis for considering some of the benefits that can be achieved and some of the mistakes that can be made when using common process-based IT service management frameworks:

Benefits to the customer/user:
- The provision of IT services becomes more customer-focused and agreements about service quality improve the relationship.
- The services are described better, in customer language, and in more appropriate detail.
- Better management of the quality, availability, reliability and cost of the services are managed better.
- Communication with the IT organization is improved by agreeing on the points of contact.

Benefits to the IT organization:

- The IT organization develops a clearer structure, becomes more efficient, and is more focused on the corporate objectives.
- The IT organization is more in control of the infrastructure and services it has responsibility for, and changes become easier to manage.
- An effective process structure provides a framework for the effective outsourcing of elements of the IT services.
- Following best practices encourages a cultural change towards providing service, and supports the introduction of quality management systems based on the ISO 9000 series or on ISO/IEC 20000.
- Frameworks can provide coherent frames of reference for internal communication and communication with suppliers, and for the standardization and identification of procedures.

Potential problems/mistakes:

- The introduction can take a long time and require significant effort, and may require a change of culture in the organization; an overambitious introduction can lead to frustration because the objectives are never met.
- If process structures become an objective in themselves, the service quality may be adversely affected; in this scenario, unnecessary or over-engineered procedures are seen as bureaucratic obstacles, which are to be avoided where possible.
- There is no improvement in IT services due a fundamental lack of understanding about what the relevant processes should provide, what the appropriate performance indicators are, and how processes can be controlled.
- Improvement in the provision of services and cost reductions are insufficiently visible, because no baseline data was available for comparison and/or the wrong targets were identified.
- A successful implementation requires the involvement and commitment of personnel at all levels in the organization; leaving the development of the process structures to a specialist department may isolate that department in the organization and it may set a direction that is not accepted by other departments.
- If there is insufficient investment in appropriate training and support tools, justice will not be done to the processes and the service will not be improved; additional resources and personnel may be needed in the short term if the organization is already overloaded by routine IT service management activities which may not be using "best practices".

2.5 Service Lifecycle: concept and overview

The information provision role and system has grown and changed since the launch of ITIL version 2 (in 2000/02). IT supports and is part of an increasing number of goods and services. In the business world, the information provision role has changed as well: IT's role is no longer just supporting, but has become the baseline for the creation of business value.

ITIL version 3 intends to include and provide insight into IT's new role in all its complexity and dynamics. To that end, a new service management approach has been chosen that does not center around processes, but focuses on the Service Lifecycle.

Basic concepts

Before we describe the Service Lifecycle, we need to define some basic concepts.

Good practice

ITIL is presented as a good practice (literally: correct method). This is an approach or method that has proven itself in practice. These good practices can be a solid backing for organizations that want to improve their IT services. In such cases, the best thing to do is to select a generic standard or method that is accessible to everyone, ITIL, CobiT, CMMI, PRINCE2® and ISO/IEC 20000, for example. One of the benefits of these freely accessible generic standards is that they can be applied to several real-life environments and situations. There is also ample training available for open standards. This makes it much easier to train staff.

Another source for good practice is proprietary knowledge. A disadvantage of this kind of knowledge is that it may be customized for the context and needs of a specific organization. Therefore, it may be difficult to adopt or replicate and it may not be as effective in use.

Service

A service is about creating value for the customer. ITIL defines a service as follows:

> A **service** is a means of delivering value to customers by facilitating outcomes the customers want to achieve without the ownership of specific costs or risks.

Outcomes are possible from the performance of tasks, and they are limited by a number of constraints. Services enhance performance and reduce the pressure of constraints. This increases the chances of the desired outcomes being realized.

Value

Value is the core of the service concept. From the customer's perspective value consists of two core components: utility and warranty. Utility is what the customer receives, and warranty is how it is provided.

Service management

ITIL defines service management as follows:

> **Service management** is a set of specialized organizational capabilities for providing value to customers in the form of services.

ITIL discusses some of the fundamental principles of service management that supplement the functions and processes in the ITIL core books. The next principles may help design a service management system:

- **Specialization & coordination** - The goal of service management is to make capabilities and resources available through services that are useful and acceptable to the customer with regard to quality, costs and risks. The service provider takes the weight of responsibility and resource management off the customer's shoulders so that they can focus on the business' core competence. Service management coordinates the business of service management responsibility with regard to certain resources. *Utility* and *warranty* act as a guide.
- **Agency principle** - Service management always involves an agent and a principal that seconds this agent to fulfill activities on their behalf. Agents may be consultants, advisors or service providers. Service agents act as intermediary between service providers and customers in conjunction with users. Usually, these agents are the service provider's staff, but they can also be self-service systems and processes for users. Value for the customer is created through agreements between principals and agents.
- **Encapsulation** - The customer's interest focuses on the value of use; he prefers to be spared from any technical details and structure complexity. The "encapsulation principle" is focused on hiding what the customer does not need and showing what is valuable and useful to the customer. Three principles are closely linked to this:
  - separation of concerns
  - modularity: a clear, modular structure
  - loose coupling: reciprocal independence of resources and users

Systems

ITIL describes the organizational structure concepts which proceed from system theory. The Service Lifecycle in ITIL version 3 is a system; however, a function, a process or an organization is a system as well. The definition of a system:

> A **system** is a group of interacting, interrelating, or interdependent components that form a unified whole, operating together for a common purpose.

Feedback and learning are two key aspects in the performance of systems; they turn processes, functions and organizations into dynamic systems. Feedback can lead to learning and growth, not only within a process, but also within an organization in its entirety.

Within a process, for instance, the feedback about the performance of one cycle is, in its turn, input for the next process cycle. Within organizations, there can be feedback between processes, functions and lifecycle phases. Behind this feedback is the common goal: the customer's objectives.

Functions and processes

The distinction between functions and processes is important in ITIL.

What is a function?

> A **function** is a subdivision of an organization that is specialized in fulfilling a specified type of work, and is responsible for specific end results.
> Functions are independent subdivisions with capabilities and resources that are required for their performance and results. They have their own practices and their own knowledge body.

What is a process?

> A **process** is a structured set of activities designed to accomplish a defined objective.
> Processes result in a goal-oriented change, and utilize feedback for self-enhancing and self-corrective actions.

Processes possess the following characteristics:
- They are **measurable** because they are performance-oriented.
- They have **specific results**.
- They provide results to **customers** or stakeholders.
- They **respond to a specific event** - a process is indeed continual and iterative, but is always originating from a certain event.

It can be difficult to determine whether something is a function or a process. According to ITIL, whether it is a function or process depends completely on the organizational design. A good example of a function is a service desk, a good example of a process is change management.

The hierarchical structure of functions can lead to the rise of "silos" in which each function is very self-oriented. This does not benefit the success of the organization as a whole. Processes run through the hierarchical structure of functions; functions often share some processes. This is how processes suppress the rise of functional silos, and help to ensure an improved coordination in between functions.

The Service Lifecycle

ITIL version 3 approaches service management from the lifecycle of a service. The Service Lifecycle is an organization model providing insight into:
- the way service management is structured
- the way the various lifecycle components are linked to each other
- the impact that changes in one component will have on other components and on the entire lifecycle system

So the new ITIL version focuses on the Service Lifecycle, and the way service management components are linked. The processes are also discussed (both the old familiar ones and the new ones) in the cycle phases. They describe how things change.

The Service Lifecycle consists of five phases. Each volume of the new ITIL books describes one of these phases:
1. **Service Strategy** - the phase of designing, developing and implementing service management as a strategic resource
2. **Service Design** - the design phase of developing appropriate IT services, including architecture, processes, policy and documents; the design goal is to meet the current and future business requirements
3. **Service Transition** - the phase of developing and improving capabilities for the transition of new and modified services to production

4. **Service Operation** - the phase of achieving effectiveness and efficiency in providing and supporting services in order to ensure value for the customer and the service provider

5. **Continual Service Improvement** - the phase of creating and maintaining the value for the customer by design improvement, and service introduction and operation

Service Strategy is the axis of the Service Lifecycle (Figure 2.3) that "runs" all other phases; it is the phase of policymaking and objectives. The phases Service Design, Service Transition and Service Operation implement this strategy, their continual theme is adjustment and change. The Continual Service Improvement phase stands for learning and improving, and embraces all cycle phases. This phase initiates improvement programs and projects, and prioritizes them based on the strategic objectives of the organization.

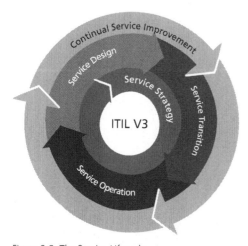

Figure 2.3 The Service Lifecycle

The Service Lifecycle is a combination of many perspectives on the reality of organizations. This offers more flexibility and control.

The dominant pattern in the Service Lifecycle is the succession of Service Strategy to Service Design, to Service Transition and to Service Operation, and then, through Continual Service Improvement, back to Service Strategy, and so on. The cycle encompasses, however, many patterns. Depending on tasks and responsibilities, a manager can choose his own control perspective. If you are responsible for the design, development or improvement of processes, the best perspective to use is a process perspective. If you are responsible for managing SLAs, contracts and services, the Service Lifecycle perspective and its various phases is likely to meet your needs better.

ITIL Library

The official, new style ITIL Library encompasses the following components:
- Core Library - the five Service Lifecycle publications:
  - Service Strategy
  - Service Design
  - Service Transition
  - Service Operation
  - Continual Service Improvement

Each book covers a phase from the Service Lifecycle and encompasses various processes. The processes are always described in detail in the book in which they find their key application.
- Complementary portfolio:
  - introduction guide
  - key element guides
  - qualification aids
  - white papers
  - glossary

CHAPTER 3

Lifecycle Phase: Service Design

3.1 Introduction

Objective

Service Design follows the Service Strategy in the Service Lifecycle, and deals with the design and development of services and their related processes. It refers not only to completely new services, but also to modified service delivery.

According to ITIL, the most important objective of Service Design is:

> *The design of new or modified services for introduction into a production environment.*

The objectives of Service Design include, but are not limited to:
- to contribute to the business objectives
- where possible, to contribute to saving time and money
- to minimize or prevent risks
- to contribute to satisfying the current and future market needs
- to assess and improve the effectiveness and efficiency of IT services
- to support the development of policies and standards regarding IT services
- to contribute to the quality of IT services

In order to ensure that the services that are developed meet the customer's expectations, the following actions must be undertaken:

- The new service must be added right from the concept phase of the service portfolio and it must be kept up-to-date throughout the process.
- The Service Level Requirements (SLR) must be clear before the service is delivered.
- Based on the SLRs, the capacity management team can model these requirements within the existing infrastructure.
- If it appears that a new infrastructure is needed or more support is desired, then financial management must be involved.
- Before the implementation phase begins, a Business Impact Analysis (BIA) and a risk assessment must be performed. This will provide valuable information for IT Service Continuity Management (ITSCM), availability management and capacity management.
- The service desk must be brought up to speed regarding the new service delivery before the new services are delivered.
- Service Transition can make a plan for the implementation of the service.
- Supplier management must be involved if there are purchases to be made.

To satisfy the changing needs and demands of the business, the design of effective and efficient IT services is a process of balancing among functionality, available resources (human, technical, and financial) and available time. This is a continual process in all phases of the lifecycle of IT services.

The Service Design phase in the lifecycle begins with the demand for new or modified requirements from the customer. Ultimately at the end of the design process, a service solution must be designed that satisfies the requirements before including the service in the transition process. Good preparation and an effective and efficient infusion of personnel, processes, products (services, technology and tools) and partners - ITIL's four Ps - is a must if the design plans and projects are to succeed.

Considering the mutual dependence of departments, IT services cannot be designed, transitioned or implemented in isolation. And everyone in the organization must be informed of the underlying components and mutual relationships of IT service delivery (and the related involved departments). This process requires a holistic approach, clear communication and the requirement that everyone can have access to the correct, most recent and unambiguous IT plans, and be provided with the appropriate information.

Design aspects

In order for the organization to strive to attain the highest possible quality with a continual "improvement focus", a structured and results-oriented approach is necessary in each of the five separate aspects of design. Results-oriented in this case means aiming "to satisfy the wishes of the customers/users." These five aspects are as follows:

1. **service solution** (including functional requirements, resources and capacities)
2. **service portfolio** (support systems and tools)
3. **architecture** (technological and management)
4. **processes**
5. **measurement systems and metrics**

1. The design of service solutions

A structured design approach is necessary in order to produce a new service for the right costs, functionality, quality and within the right time frame. The process must be iterative and incremental in order to satisfy the customers' changing wishes and requirements. The following matters should be taken into consideration:

- analysis of agreed business requirements
- revision of existing IT services and infrastructures and development of alternative services
- design of the services on the basis of new requirements
- the contents of the Service Acceptance Criteria (SAC) must be included in the initial design
- evaluation of costs of alternatives
- agreed expenditures and costs
- evaluation and confirmation of benefits for the business
- decide on the desired solutions, results and objectives (SLR)
- monitor the services in light of the overall strategies
- ensure that corporate and IT governance and security controls are satisfied
- ensure that the service functions effectively and satisfies the requirements
- support agreements are necessary to deliver the service
- assemble the Service Design Package (SDP); this includes all aspects of the service and the requirements for all successive stages in the lifecycle

2. The design of the service portfolio

The service portfolio is the most critical management system for supporting all of the processes. It describes the service delivery in terms of value for the customer and must include all of the service information and its status. In any event, the portfolio gives a definitive answer regarding the phase in which the service takes place. The following is an overview of the service portfolio, highlighting the various phases. It is important to note that the customer has an insight only into the service catalogue, see Figure 3.1. The other sections of the portfolio are not available to the customer.

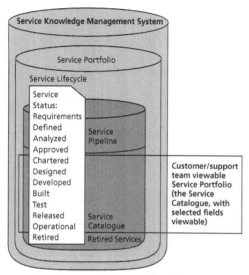

Figure 3.1 Content of the service portfolio

Although the service portfolio is designed during the Service Design phase (see the service catalogue management process), the portfolio is managed by the Service Strategy.

3. The design of the architecture

The architecture design activities include preparing the blueprints for the development and deployment of an IT infrastructure, the applications and data (according to the needs of the business). It should be noted that during this design aspect, the provision of quality, high value services is possible only by the personnel, the processes and the partners that are involved in this production aspect. ITIL describes this architecture design as follows:

> **Architecture design** is the development and maintenance of IT policy, strategies, architectures, designs, documents, plans and processes for deployment, implementation and improvement of appropriate IT services and solutions throughout the organization.

The design of an architecture is not simple and varying - sometimes conflicting - needs must be taken into account. In any case, it must be ensured that:
- it satisfies the needs of the business, its products and services
- a proper balance is found among innovation, risks and costs
- it conforms to relevant frameworks, strategies, policies, etc.
- there is coordination among the designers, planners, strategists, etc.

Every enterprise is a complex system of functions, processes, structures and information sources. The architecture of the enterprise must offer insights into how these matters connect with each other in order to achieve the enterprise objectives. The enterprise architecture is, in its own right, equally large and complex.

There are various frameworks for the development of enterprise architectures. The enterprise architecture must include the following elements:
- **service architecture** - translates the applications, infrastructure, organization and support activities into services to the business
- **application architecture** - ensures the development of blueprints for the development of individual applications
- **information architecture** - describes how the information sources are managed and distributed
- **IT infrastructure architecture** - describes the structure, function and geographic distribution of hardware and software
- **environment architecture** - describes all of the aspects, types and levels of the environment controls

In addition to a technical component (applications, system software, information and data, infrastructure and environment systems), a management architecture must also be developed. In this regard, there are five elements that must be taken into consideration, namely: the sector (needs, requirements), personnel, processes, tools and technology (IT products that are used in providing the services). It is important that the technology is not the primary focus, but rather the wishes and requirements of the customer.

4. The design of processes
Working with defined processes is the basis of ITIL. By defining what the activities are and what the input and output are, it is possible to work more efficiently and effectively, and especially in a more customer-oriented way. By assessing these processes, the organization can enhance its efficiency and effectiveness even further. The next step is to establish norms and standards. In this way the organization can link the quality

requirements with the output. This approach corresponds with Deming's *Plan-Do-Check-Act* Management Cycle.

Every process must have a process owner who is responsible for the process and for its improvement. Service Design offers the process owner support in the design process by standardizing terms and templates and ensuring that processes are consistent and are integrated.

ITIL describes a process as follows:

> A **process** is a structured set of activities designed to achieve a specific goal. A process makes defined outputs out of one or more inputs. A process includes all roles, responsibilities; resources and management controls that are needed to deliver reliable output and can possibly define policy, standards, guidelines, activities, procedures and work instructions, if necessary.

A process consists of the implementation of activities and the monitoring of that implementation. Process control is defined further as:

> **Process control** consists of the planning and regulation of a process, with the purpose of executing that process in an efficient, effective and consistent manner.

5. The design of measurement systems and metrics
In order to lead and manage the development process effectively, regular assessments must be performed. The selected assessment system must be synchronized with the capacity and maturity of the processes that are assessed. Care should be taken as it will affect the behavior of delivering the service. Immature processes are not capable of supporting refined assessments. There are four elements that can be investigated, namely **progress**, **fulfillment**, **effectiveness** and **efficiency** of the process. As the processes develop over time, the units of measure also must develop. Therefore, the emphasis in mature processes is more on the assessment of efficiency and effectiveness.

Value of Service Design
Good Service Design offers the following benefits:
*   lower Total Cost of Ownership (TCO)

- improved quality of service delivery
- improved consistency of the service
- simpler implementation of new or modified services
- improved synchronization of services with the needs of the business
- improved effectiveness of performances
- improved IT administration
- more effective service management and IT processes
- more simplified decision-making

Design constraints and opportunities

Although designers are free to design services, it must be understood that they are dependent on internal resources (including available financial resources) and external circumstances (e.g. the impact of ISO, SOX and COBIT). In addition, the design process offers opportunities to enhance the effectiveness and efficiency of IT facilities through the use of a Service Oriented Architecture (SOA) approach, considering the resulting decrease in time for delivering service solutions to the business.

It is important that the services are kept up-to-date in the service catalogue (part of the service portfolio and the configuration management system, or CMS). In general, this will position the organization to link IT facilities with the objectives (business service management). This will allow them to predict the impact of technology on the business and vice versa.

Business Service Management (BSM) enables the organization to:
- synchronize IT facilities with the business objectives
- set the priorities of IT activities on the basis of their impact on the business
- increase productivity and profitability
- support "corporate governance"
- enhance competitive advantages
- increase the quality of service delivery and customer satisfaction

3.2   Basic concepts

Service Design models

Which model should be used for the development of IT services largely depends on the model that is chosen for the delivery of IT services. Before a new design model is adopted, an overview of the available IT capacities and equipment should be made.

This overview should focus on the following elements:
- business drivers and demands
- the scope and capability of the current service provider
- the requirements and goals of the new service
- the scope and capability of current external service providers
- the maturity of the organizations and their processes
- the culture of the organizations
- IT infrastructure, applications, data, services and other components
- the level of corporate and IT governance
- available budget and resources
- staff levels and available skills

Insights into the above issues will help determine what the opportunities for the organization are and whether they are in a position to take the next step of providing new or changed services. The manner in which the next step is taken should be based on the business drivers and on the capabilities of the IT organization (and its partners).

Delivery options for IT services
The gap (between the current and the desired situation) does not necessarily have to be bridged by the organization itself. There are various strategies that can be considered for outsourcing some or all of the services, each with advantages and disadvantages. The most common of these are summarized in Table 3.1.

The choice of one of the above delivery strategies depends on the specific situation in which the organization finds itself. Various issues play a role in the decision. The organization's available internal capacities and needs and the personnel (culture) have a significant impact on the delivery strategy. Whichever strategy is chosen, it is always essential to assess and review the performances in order to remain ultimately able to satisfy the changing demands of the market.

Design- and development options for IT services
In order to make the appropriate decision regarding the design and delivery of IT services, it is crucial to understand the current lifecycle stages, methods and approaches for service development. Insights into the following aspects of lifecycle approaches for service development are essential:
- the structure (milestones)
- activities (work flows, tasks)
- primary models associated with the chosen method giving various perspectives (process-, data-, event- and users' perspectives)

Delivery strategy	Characteristics	Advantages	Disadvantages
in-sourcing	Internal capacities are used for the design, development, maintenance, execution, and/or offer of support for the service.	- direct control - freedom of choice - familarity with internal processes	- cost and time for delivering services - dependence on internal resources and competencies
outsourcing	Engaging an external organization for the design, development, maintenance, execution, and/or offering of support of the service.	- focus on care competencies - reducing long-term costs	- less direct control - unfamiliarity with the skills of the supplier
co-sourcing	A combination of in- and outsourcing in which various outsourcing organizations work co-operatively throughout the lifecycle.	- time to deliver services - better control	- complexity of projects - intellectual property and copyright protection
multi-sourcing	Multiple organizations make formal agreements with the focus on strategic partnerships (creating new market opportunities).	- expanded market opportunities - competitive response opportunities	- complexity of projects - 'culture clash'
business process outsourcing (BPO)	An external organization takes over a business process, or part of one, at a chapter location, e.g. a call center.	- one-counter functionality - access to specialized skills	- loss of knowledge - loss of relationship with the business
application service provision	Computer-based services are offered to the customer over a network.	- access to complex and expensive solutions - support and upgrades included	- access only to facilities, not knowledge - 'culture clash'
knowledge process outsourcing (KPO)	This goes one step further than BPO, and rather than offering knowledge of a (part of a) process, knowledge of an entire work area is offered.	- knowledge and expertise - cost savings	- loss of internal knowledge - loss of relationship with the business

Table 3.1 IT services delivery strategies

Rapid Application Development

It is necessary to understand the differences between object-oriented and structured system development and the basic principles of Rapid Application Development (RAD) in order to recognize how the choice of a software solution changes the structure of the lifecycle approach.

Traditional development approaches are based on the principle that the requirements of the customer/client can be determined at the beginning of the lifecycle and that the development costs can be kept under control by managing the changes. RAD-approaches begin with the notion that change is inevitable and that discouraging change simply indicates passivity in regard to the market. The RAD-approach is an incremental and iterative development approach.

The incremental approach implies that a service is designed bit by bit. Parts are developed separately and are delivered piecemeal. Each piece is supported by one of the business functions and together they support the whole. The big advantage in this approach is its shorter delivery time. The development of each part, however, requires that all phases of the lifecycle are continued.

The iterative approach implies that the lifecycle is repeated many times through the design. Prototypes of the entire process are used in order to understand the customer-specific requirements better, after which the design is adapted to it.

A combination of the two approaches is possible. An organization can begin by specifying the requirements for the entire service, followed by an incremental design and the development of the application.

RAD-approaches, such as the Unified Process and the Dynamic Systems Development Method (DSDM), are a response to the customer's demand to keep costs low during the development project. Thus DSDM involves the user in the development process of developing a software system that satisfies the expectations (demands) that can be adjusted, for on-time delivery within the allotted budget.

RAD-approaches not only provide a substantial savings in time, they also reduce development and implementation risks. Although they might be more difficult to manage than conventional approaches and involve more requirements regarding the skills and experience of the personnel, they make a positive contribution to the implementation and overall acceptance in the organization. They also support developers to anticipate changing organization demands more quickly, so that they can modify the design. Contrary to traditional approaches, the RAD-teams are smaller and are made up of generalists. In addition, it is easier to insert critical decisions during the process.

Commercial of the shelf solutions
Many organizations choose standard software solutions to satisfy needs and demands. A framework is needed for the selection, modification and implementation of packages of

this kind, and it is especially important to know at the outset what requirements are set at management and operational levels. It is equally important in regard to purchasing, to have an understanding of the advantages and disadvantages of such packages.

Besides defining the functional requirements, it is also crucial to determine the requirements in regard to the product, the supplier and the integration of the service package.

3.3   Processes and other activities

Processes

In this section is a description of Service Design processes and activities that are responsible for the delivery of important information for the design of a new or changed service solution. A results-oriented, structured approach, together with consideration of the five aforementioned design aspects, guarantees service delivery of the highest quality and consistency in the organization as a whole. A more extensive description of the processes can be found in Chapter 5 of this book.

All of the design activities in this phase of the lifecycle stem from the needs and demands of the customer and are a reflection of the strategy, planning and policy produced by the Service Strategy. Each phase of the lifecycle is input for the following phase of the lifecycle. Service Strategy provides important input into the Service Design, which in turn provides input for the Transition phase. Therefore it is, in fact, the backbone of the Service Lifecycle.

In order to develop effective and efficient services that satisfy the customers' needs, it is essential that the output from the other areas and processes be included in the Service Design process. The seven tightly connected processes in the Service Design phase are:
- service catalogue management
- service level management
- capacity management
- availability management
- IT service continuity management
- information security management
- supplier management

Service Catalogue Management (SCM)

Service catalogue management is an important component of the service portfolio. The two comprise the backbone of the Service Lifecycle by providing information to every other phase. Although the overall portfolio is produced as a component of the Service Strategy, it needs the cooperation of all of the successive phases. At the moment that a service is ready for use, the Service Design produces the specifications that can be included in the service portfolio. The ultimate goal of service catalogue Management is the development and maintenance of a service catalogue that includes all of the accurate details and the status of all existing services and business processes they support, as well as those in development. It comprises, thus, the portion of the portfolio that is visible to the customer.

Service Level Management (SLM)

Service level management represents the IT service provider to the customer, and the customer internally to the IT service provider. The goal of this process is to take responsibility for ensuring that the levels of IT service delivery are achieved, both for existing services and future services in accordance with the agreed targets. SLM includes the planning, coordinating, providing, agreeing, monitoring and reporting of service level agreements (SLAs), including the revision of attained service delivery, to ensure that the quality satisfies, and where possible, exceeds, the agreed requirements. An SLA is a written established agreement between a service provider and a customer that records the goals and responsibilities of both parties. This process supports the service catalogue Management by providing information and trends regarding customer satisfaction.

Capacity management

Capacity management is the central point for all designs regarding IT performance and capacity issues. The goal of capacity management is to ensure that the capacity corresponds to both the existing and future needs of the customer (recorded in a capacity plan). The engine behind the process of capacity management is the requirements that the customer poses and that are recorded in the SLA.

Synchronization between capacity management and the service portfolio and SLM within the lifecycle of Service Design is essential. Thus capacity management provides information on existing and future resources through which the organization can decide which components will be renewed and when and how that will be done. For its part, capacity management must also have a view regarding the plans of the organization as outlined in the IT Service Strategy.

Availability management

The availability and reliability of IT services have a direct influence on customer satisfaction and the reputation of the service provider. Availability management is, therefore, essential and must be involved at an early stage in the lifecycle, just as is the case with capacity management. Availability management includes the entire process of designing, implementing, assessing, managing and improving IT services and the components included therein. The goal of this process is to ensure that the availability level of both new and modified services corresponds with the levels as agreed with the customer. In order to achieve that, availability management can implement both proactive and reactive activities that include monitoring and reporting of the availability metrics, and must maintain the availability management information system, which includes all of the necessary information, and this forms the basis of the availability plan.

IT Service Continuity Management (ITSCM)
IT service continuity management plays a valuable role in the support of the process of business continuity planning. This process can be applied by organizations as a means of focusing attention on continuity and recovery requirements, and to justify the decision to implement a business continuity plan. The ultimate goal of ITSCM is to support business continuity by ensuring that the required IT facilities can be restored within the agreed time. The process focuses on occurrences that can be considered as disasters (calamities). The focus in the first instance is solely on IT-related matters that support the business processes. Less significant catastrophes will be handled through the incident management process.

Information security management
Information security management ensures that the information security policy satisfies the organization's overall security policy and the requirements originating from corporate governance.

Security is not really a step in the lifecycle. Information security is a continual process and is an integral component of all of the services. This process supports the consciousness of the entire organization in regard to service delivery. Information security management must understand the entire playing field of IT and business security so that it is in a position to manage existing and future security aspects of the business. The Information security management system (ISMS) serves as the basis for a cost-effective development of an information security program that supports the business objectives.

Supplier management
The process of supplier management draws attention to all of the suppliers and contracts in order to support the delivery of services to the customer. The goal is to guarantee a constant level of quality for the right price. All activities in this process stem from the suppliers strategy and the policy originating with the Service Strategy. In order to achieve

consistency and effectiveness during the implementation of the policy, a suppliers and contracts database must be established which includes suppliers and contracts as well as the execution of the supported services. All of this should be done with an eye towards valuable, high-quality IT service delivery. The supplier management process must be "in sync" with the demands of the organization as well as the requirements of information security management and ITSCM.

Activities
In addition to the seven processes mentioned earlier, three activities can be differentiated in Service Design. They are:
* development of requirements
* data- and information management
* application management

Development of requirements

Type of requirements
ITIL assumes that the analysis of the existing and required business processes results in functional requirements that fall under IT services (consisting of applications, data, infrastructure, environment and skills).
There are three types of requirements for each system, namely:
* **Functional requirements** - These describe matters for which a service could be done and that can be expressed as a task or function of which a component must be carried out. Various models can be considered for specifying the functional requirements, such as:
  - system context diagram
  - use case model
* **Management- and operational requirements** - These define the non-functional requirements of the IT service. The requirements serve as a basis for the first systems, the estimation of costs and support for the viability of the proposed service. Requirements from the management and execution can relate to a large number of quality aspects:
  - manageability
  - efficiency
  - availability and reliability
  - capacity and performance
  - security
  - installation
  - continuity

- controllability
- maintainability
- operability
- measurability and reportability
- **Usability requirements** - Ensure that the services satisfy the expectations of the users in terms of ease of use and user friendliness. In order to achieve this, the following must be done:
  - develop performance standards for evaluations
  - define test scenarios

Just as with management- and operational requirements, usability requirements can be adopted to test applications for compliance with the usability requirements.

Requirement investigation
There are various investigation techniques for arriving at clearer requirements. Considering that customers are often unsure about the requirements, the support of a developer is sometimes necessary. This person must be aware of the fact that people may see him/her as "someone from the IT department", which dictates the requirements. A certain amount of care is therefore called for. Possible investigation methods are:

- interviews
- workshops
- observation
- protocol analysis
- shadowing
- scenario analysis
- prototyping

Problems in the development of requirements
There are various problems that can occur in developing requirements:

- lack of relevance to the objectives of the service
- lack of clarity or ambiguity in the wording
- duplication between requirements
- conflicts between requirements
- uncertainty on the part of users
- inconsistent levels of detail

In order to face these and other problems, it is important to appoint participants. Three groups need to be involved in the establishment of requirements:

- the customer

- the users' community
- the service development team

Documenting requirements
The requirements document is the core of the process. This document contains every individual requirement in a standard template. The requirements that eventually come from the users must also be included. Every requirement must be SMART (Specific, Measureable, Achievable/Appropriate, Realistic/Relevant and Timely/Time-bound) formulated. In addition, they should be checked to make sure they are clear, unambiguous and reasonable, synchronized with the customer's objectives, and not in conflict with any of the other requirements.

The result can then be recorded in the requirements catalogue. This should be a component of the requirements portfolio in the overall service portfolio. The users' requirements should be included here and labeled with an identification number, the source, the owner, the priority (e.g. according to the MoSCoW-approach: must have, should have, could have, won't have), description, involved business process, and so on.

The requirements analysis is an iterative process. In other words, the requirements change during the course of the development process of the service. It is therefore also important that the users be involved throughout the entire process.

Data- and information management
Data is one of the most critical matters that must be kept under control in order to develop, deliver and support effective IT services. Factors for successful data management include:

- the users have access to the information that they need for their work
- information is shared in the organization
- the quality of the information is maintained at an acceptable level
- legal aspects in the areas of privacy, security and confidentiality are taken into account

If data assets are not effectively managed, there is a risk that people will collect information and data that are not necessary; emphasis will be placed on outdated information; a lot of information is no longer accessible; and information is made accessible to those who are not authorized to have it.

Scope

There are four management areas in the field of data and information management:

- **Management of data sources** - The sources should be clear and responsibilities must be entrusted to the right person. This process is also known as data administration. This activity includes the following responsibilities:
    - define the need for information
    - a data inventory and an enterprise data model must be developed
    - identify shortages and ambiguities
    - maintain a catalogue
    - assess the costs and the rewards of the organization data
- **Management of data- and information technology** - This area relates to the management of IT and includes matters such as the design of databases and database management.
- **Management of information processes** - The data lifecycle (process of creating, collecting, accessing, modifying, storing, deleting and archiving of data) must be controlled. This often occurs in conjunction with the application management process.
- **Management of data standards and policy** - The organization must formulate standards and policy for data management as a component of the IT strategy.

Data management and the Service Lifecycle

In order to understand the use of data in business processes, it is recommended that a lifecycle approach be followed that looks into subjects such as:

- What data do we have at this time and how are they classified?
- What data should be collected through the business processes?
- How will the data be stored and maintained?
- How are the data accessed and by whom?
- How are the data disposed of and by whom?
- How is the data quality protected?
- How can the data be made more accessible and available?

Data has an important connotation; not only for organizations for which the provision of data is a core business; consider, for example, a press bureau such as Reuters. Data is increasingly viewed as a common property with a value that can be placed in financial terms. Various opportunities for this exist:

- **Valuing data by its availability** - This approach looks at which business processes would not be possible if a certain portion of the data were not available, and what this would cost the organization.

- **Valuing lost data** - This approach examines the cost of having to replace data if it were lost or destroyed.
- **Valuing data by considering the data lifecycle** - This approach focuses on issues such as how data is created; how it is made available; and how it is archived; the lifecycle differs (and thus, so do the costs) depending on the demand, or if these steps can be performed by an internal or external party.

Classifying data

Data can be classified on three levels:

- **Operational data** - This data is necessary for the continued functioning of the organization and is the least specific.
- **Tactical data** - This is data that is needed for line- or higher management; among other things, this refers to quarterly data, distilled from management information systems.
- **Strategic data** - Refers to the long-term trends compared with external (market) information.

Data owner

Responsibilities of the data owner include:

- determining who can create, revise, read and delete data
- consent given regarding the way in which data are stored for modification
- approves level of security
- agreeing business description and a purpose

Data integrity

In defining IT services, it is important that management and operational data requirements be considered. Specifically in the following areas:

- restoration of lost data
- controlled access to data
- implementation of policy on archiving of data
- periodic monitoring of data integrity

Application management

An application is defined by ITIL as:

> An **application** is a software program(s) with specific functions that offer direct support to the execution of business processes and/or procedures.

Applications, along with data and infrastructure, comprise the technical component of IT services. It is crucial that the applications that are provided correspond with the requirements of the customer. Organizations often expend a great deal of time on the functional requirements of the new service, while too little time is spent on the design of the management- and operational (non-functional) requirements of the service. That means that when the service is performed, it completely caters to the functional requirements, but not to the expectations of the business and the customer in the area of quality and performance.

Two alternative approaches are necessary to implement application management, namely:
- **Service Development Lifecycle** - (SDLC) is a systematic problem-solving approach for supporting the development of an IT service. This consists of the following steps:
  - feasibility study
  - analysis
  - design
  - testing
  - implementation
  - evaluation
  - maintenance
- **Application maintenance** - The other approach looks globally at all of the services in order to ensure a continuing process of managing and maintaining the applications. All applications are described consistently in the application portfolio, which is synchronized with the customers' requirements.

Application frameworks
The application framework includes all management- and operational aspects and provides solutions for all of the management- and operational requirements for an application.

Architecture-related activities must be planned and managed separately from the individual system-based software projects. Application designers must concentrate on one application, while application framework developers focus on more than one application and on the opportunities.

A method which is often employed is to distinguish between different types of applications. For example, not every application can be used on a Microsoft Windows platform, coupled with a UNIX server in which HTML, Java-applets and JavaBeans must be used. The different application types can be viewed as an application family. Every application in the same family is based on the same application framework.

In this concept the first step of the application design phase is the identification of the right framework. As the application framework matures, various decisions can be made. If it is not mature then the right strategy is to collect and analyze the requirements that do not fit with the existing framework. Based on the application requirements, new requirements can be defined for the application framework, after which the framework can be modified so that it satisfies all of the requirements.

CASE tools
An aspect of overall alignment is the need to align applications with their underlying support structures. Development environments traditionally have their own Computer Assisted/Aided Software Engineering tools (CASE) that, for example, offer the means to specify requirements, draw design diagrams or generate applications. They are also a location for storage and for managing the elements that are created.

Application development
After the design phase, the application must be further developed. Both the application and the environment must be prepared for the launch. The application development phase includes the following issues:
- consistent coding conventions
- independent structural guidelines for applications
- business-ready testing
- management checklist for the building phase
- organization of the team roles for the structure

Important outputs of application development include:
- scripts for starting and stopping an application
- scripts for monitoring both hardware- and software configurations
- specifications of the unit of measure that can be obtained from the application
- SLA-objectives and requirements
- operational requirements and documentation
- support requirements

3.4   Organization

Roles and responsibilities

Well performing organizations can quickly and accurately make the right decisions and execute them successfully. In order to achieve this, it is crucial that the roles and responsibilities are clearly defined. This is also an essential issue in the Service Design process. One of the possible models that can be helpful in this regard is the RACI model. RACI is an acronym for the four most important roles:

* **Responsible** - the person who is responsible for completing the task
* **Accountable** - just one person who is accountable for each task
* **Consulted** - people who give advice
* **Informed** - people who must be kept in the loop regarding the progress of the project

In establishing a RACI system, the following steps are necessary:
* identify activities and processes
* identify and define functional roles
* conduct meetings and delegate the RACI-codes
* identify gaps and potential overlaps
* distribute the chart and build in feedback
* ensure that the allocations are followed

Skills

Despite the fact that every position brings with it specific skills and competencies (see "Roles" below), the responsible person must:
* be aware of the business priorities and objectives
* be aware of the role that IT plays
* possess customer service skills
* be aware of what IT can provide to the customer
* have the competencies and knowledge that are needed in order to perform the function well
* have ability to use, understand and interpret the best practice policies and procedures to ensure adherence

Roles

In this section is a description of the roles and responsibilities of the most important positions in the Service Design process. Depending on the size of organizations these roles can be combined. The most important roles are:

- **The process owner** is responsible for ensuring that the process is implemented as agreed and that the established objectives will therefore be achieved. Tasks are:
  - documenting and recording the process
  - defining the KPIs and if necessary revising them
  - improving the effectiveness and efficiency of the process
  - providing input to the Service Improvement Plan
  - reviewing the process, the roles and responsibilities
- **The service design manager** is responsible for the overall coordination and inputting of the service designs. Tasks include:
  - ensure that the Service Strategy corresponds with the design process and that the designs satisfy the established requirements
  - design the functional aspects of the services
  - produce and maintain the design documentation
  - assess the effectiveness and efficiency of the design process
- **The service catalogue manager** is responsible for the production and maintenance of the service catalogue. In addition, the service catalogue manager must:
  - ensure that the services are recorded in the service catalogue
  - ensure that the information that has been included is up-to-date and is consistent with the information in the service portfolio
  - ensure that the catalogue is secure and that there are backups
- **The service level manager** has as their most important responsibilities to:
  - have an insight into the changing demands of the customer and the market
  - ensure that the customers' existing and future requirements have been identified
  - negotiate and make agreements on the delivery of services
  - assist in the production and maintenance of an accurate services portfolio
  - ensure that the objectives that have been ratified in underlying contracts are synchronized with the SLA
- **The availability manager** is responsible for:
  - ensuring that the existing services are available as agreed
  - assisting in investigating and diagnosing all incidents and problems
  - contributing to the design of the IT infrastructure
  - proactively improving the availability of services
- **The security manager** has as their most important tasks to:
  - design and maintain the information security policy
  - communicate with the involved parties on matters pertaining to the security policy
  - assist in the business impact analysis
  - perform risk analyses and risk management together with availability management and ITSCM

In addition, there are still the following responsible positions to recognize in this process:
- IT planner
- IT designer/architect
- service continuity manager
- capacity manager
- supplier manager

3.5 Methods, techniques and tools

Technological considerations

It is extremely important that someone ensures that the tools to be used support the processes and not the other way around. There are various tools and techniques that can be used for supporting the service and component designs. They not only make the hardware and software designs possible, but also enable the development of environment designs, process designs and data designs. The great variety of tools and techniques offer the following benefits:
- attainment of speed in the design process
- adherence to standards
- the development of prototypes and models
- take into account diverse scenarios (what if...?)

The design process can be simplified by making use of tools that give a graphic image of the service and its components; from the business processes to the service and the SLA, through the infrastructure, environment, data and applications, processes, OLAs (operational level agreements), teams, contracts and suppliers. If the tool also contains financial information and is coupled with a "metrics tree", the service can be guarded and managed through all of the phases in its lifecycle.

These tools not only facilitate the design process, they also support all of the phases in the Service Lifecycle, including:
- management of all levels of the Service Lifecycle
- all aspects of the service and the performances
- management of costs
- management of the service portfolio and catalogue
- a Configuration Management System (CMS) and a Service Knowledge Management System (SKMS)

The following generic activities must be performed:
- ensure that there is a generic lifecycle for IT assets
- formalize relationships between different types of IT assets
- define the roles and responsibilities
- ensure that a study is performed in order to understand the TCO of an IT service

Even more can be added for application assets:
- define an acquisition strategy for IT assets and analyze how this can be synchronized with both the IT- and the business strategy
- document the role that the application plays in the provision of IT services
- determine standards for the use of various approaches to the design of applications

For data/information assets still more can be added:
- ensure that data designs are made in the light of:
  - the importance of standardization
  - the need for qualitatively valuable data
  - the value of data to the organization

For IT infrastructure assets more can be added:
- establish standards for the acquisition and management of IT- and environmental infrastructure (electricity, space, middleware, database systems etc.)
- determine activities for the optimum use of the IT infrastructure assets
- specify the need for tools and describe how they would be used

For skills assets more can be added:
- formalize how competencies could be considered as assets in the organization
- ensure that the competencies are documented

In order to establish interfaces and dependencies the following can be added:
- formalize the interfaces that the acquisition and management of IT assets have with functions and processes outside the IT sphere
- formalize quality control in the acquisition and management of IT assets

Service management tools

Tools help ensure that Service Design processes can function effectively. They enhance efficiency and provide valuable management information on the identification of possible weak points. The long-term benefit is that the use of tools serves to reduce costs and increase productivity, in the interest of improving the quality of IT service delivery.

In addition, the use of tools makes possible the centralization of essential processes, as well as the automation and integration of "core" service management processes.

Considerations in the evaluation of service management tools include:
* data structure, data handling and integration
* conformity with international standards
* flexibility in implementation, use, and sharing of data
* support in the monitoring of service levels

The tool serves to support the process rather than the other way around. If possible, it is recommended that a completely integrated tool be acquired, that supports the many service management processes. If this is not possible, then interfaces among the various tools should be taken into consideration. During the selection process it is advisable to employ a Statement of Requirements (SoR). The requirements should be considered using the MoSCoW analysis:
* **M** - must have this
* **S** - should have this
* **C** - could have this
* **W** - won't have this now, but would like in the future

The tool must be flexible so that it can support individual access rights. It is necessary to determine who has access to the data and with what objective. In addition, it must be decided as to which platform the tool can work on. During the first consideration it is wise to look into the credit worthiness of the supplier and find out if they offer support (training) for a few months or years. In this process it is important to realize that a solution almost never satisfies 100% of the requirements. The 80/20 rule is perhaps more realistic in this framework. In other words, the tool is likely to satisfy closer to 80% of the established requirements.

3.6   Implementation

Implementation considerations
In the following section the implementation considerations for Service Design are addressed. In addition, the interfaces of Service Design with the other phases of the Service Lifecycle will be discussed.

Business impact analysis

The Business Impact Analysis (BIA) is a valuable source of information for establishing the customer's needs, and the impact and the risk of a service. The BIA is an essential element in the business continuity process and dictates the strategy to be followed for risk reduction and recovery after a catastrophe. The BIA consists of two parts: on the one hand is the investigation of the impact of the loss of a business process or function; on the other hand is the stopping of the effect of that loss.

The BIA must be conducted in order to support the definition of the business continuity strategy, and makes it possible to better understand the function and the importance of the service. In this way the organization can determine, among other things:
- what the critical services are
- what an acceptable time is for the service to be unavailable
- what an acceptable level of unavailability of the service is
- what the costs of the loss of the service are
- what are the critical business & service periods

Implementation of Service Design

The process, policy and architecture for the design of IT services, as described in this book, must be documented and used in order to design and implement appropriate IT services. In principle, it is recommended that all of the processes be implemented at the same time since all of the processes are related to each other and often are also dependent on each other. What is ultimately needed is an integrated set of processes that IT services can manage and oversee throughout the entire lifecycle. Since organizations can rarely implement everything at once, the process for which there is the greatest need should be the first to be done, realizing that all processes are interlinked. In addition, this also depends on the maturity of the organization's IT service management. The implementation priorities must correspond with the objectives of the Service Improvement Program (SIP). If, for example, availability of IT services is an important point, then the organization must focus on those processes that will improve availability; in this case, incident management, problem management, change management and availability management. Various other processes, such as capacity management, security management and continuity management also influence availability, as illustrated by the intertwining of the ITIL processes.

It is important that a structured project management method be used during the implementation phase. The CSI model is a good example of such a method. The success of the Service Design and the success of the improvement of the Service Design processes must be assessed. The results must then be analyzed and reported. If it does not satisfy the requirements, then an adjustment is probably needed. During the entire process assessments must be made. One of the possible methods is the Balanced Scorecard, which was developed by Robert Kaplan and David Norton as a method for measuring business activities in terms of its strategy and vision, and with which a good image of the organization's performance can be sketched.

Prerequisites
There are various prerequisites for new or revised processes. They are often requirements of other processes. For example, before Service Level Management (SLM) can design the Service Level Agreement (SLA) a business service catalogue and a technical service catalogue are necessary. Problem management depends on a mature incident management process. These things are much bigger than just ITSM: availability and capacity management need information of the business plan. There are more of these examples which need to be considered first before high process maturity can be achieved.

Critical success factors and KPIs
It is recommended that every IT service provider focuses on a number of critical success factors and KPIs. They should be determined at the beginning of the Continual Service Improvement Program.

KPIs for Service Design are:
- percentage of specifications of the requirements of Service Design produced on time
- percentage of specifications of the requirements of Service Design produced within budget
- percentage of Service Design packs produced on time
- accuracy of Service Design
- accuracy of the SLAs, OLAs and contracts

Challenges
Examples of challenges that are faced during implementation include:
- the need for synchronization of existing architecture, strategy and policy
- the use of various technologies and applications
- unclear or changing customer requirements
- lack of awareness and knowledge of service delivery
- resistance to working systematically
- inefficient use of resources

In order to overcome the challenges, consideration may be given to the following matters:
- insights into the customer's requirements and priorities
- adequate communication with involved parties, but equally, be a "listening ear"
- involve as many people as possible in the design process
- ensure the involvement of management and personnel

Risks
There are several risks during the Service Design phase, including:
- if the level of maturity in one of the processes is low, it is impossible to reach a high level of maturity in other processes
- business requirements are not clear for the IT personnel
- too little time is allotted for Service Design
- synchronization among infrastructure, customer and partners is not good, which means the requirements cannot be satisfied
- the Service Design phase is not clear or on the whole is not available

Interfaces with other phases in the lifecycle

All activities in the Service Design phase originate from the customer's needs and requirements, and are then also a reflection of the strategy, plans and policy produced by the first phase of the lifecycle: the Services Strategy.

The Service Design phase in the lifecycle begins with the new or changed requirements of the customer. Ultimately, by the end of the design process, a service solution must be designed which satisfies those requirements before they begin the transition process together with the service package. In the transition phase, the service will be evaluated, structured, tested and deployment will take place after which the implementation will be transferred to Service Operation.

Figure 3.2 makes clear that the output from every phase is input for the next phase in the lifecycle. Thus Service Strategy provides important input to Service Design, which in turn, provides input to the transition phase.

The service portfolio provides information to every process in every phase of the lifecycle. In this respect it is in fact the backbone of the Service Lifecycle. The service portfolio must be a component of the service knowledge management system and be included as a document in the configuration management system.

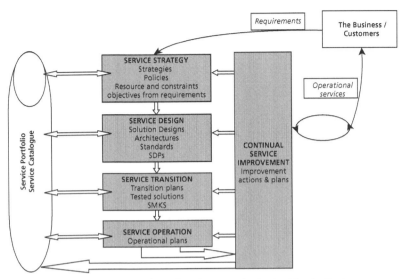

Figure 3.2 The most important relationships, inputs and outputs of Service Design

CHAPTER 4

Introduction to Functions and Processes

4.1 Introduction

Processes are *internal* affairs for the IT service provider. An organization that is still trying to gain control of its processes therefore has an **internal focus**. Organizations that focus on gaining control of their systems in order to provide services are still internally focused. The organization is not ready for an **external focus** until it controls its services and is able to vary them on request. This external focus is required to evolve into that desirable customer-focused organization.

Because organizations can be in different stages of maturity, IT managers require a broad orientation in their discipline. Most organizations are now working on the introduction of a process-focused or customer-focused approach, or still have to start working on this. Process control is therefore a vital step on the road towards a **mature customer-focused organization**.

ITIL has made an important contribution to the organization of that process-focused operating method in the past decade. The development started in North-western Europe and has made some progress on most other continents in the last few years also. On a global scale, however, a minimal number of organizations have actually started with this approach - and an even smaller number have made serious progress at this point. The organization change projects that were thought to be necessary to convert to a process-focused organization were not all successful.

These findings lead us to conclude that the majority of organizations in the world require access to good information and best practices concerning the **business processes of**

IT organizations. Fortunately, that information is abundant. The ITIL version 2 books provide comprehensive documentation on the most important processes, while ITIL version 3 adds even more information.

The **process model** is at least as important as the processes because processes must be deployed in the right relationships to achieve the desired effect of a process-focused approach. There are many different process models available. The experiences gained with these processes and process models in recent years have been documented comprehensively in books, magazines and white papers, and have been presented at countless conventions.

4.2   Management of processes

Every organization aims to realize its vision, mission, strategy, objectives and policies, which means that appropriate activities have to be undertaken.

For example, a restaurant will have to purchase fresh ingredients, the chefs will have to work together to provide consistent results, and there should be no major differences in style among the waiting staff. A restaurant will only be awarded a three-star rating when it manages to provide the same high quality over an extended period of time. This is not always the case: there will be changes among the waiting staff, a successful approach may not last, and chefs often leave to open their own restaurants. Providing consistently high quality means that the component activities have to be coordinated: the better and more efficiently the kitchen operates, the higher the quality of service that can be provided to the guests.

In the example of the restaurant, appropriate activities include buying vegetables, bookkeeping, ordering publicity material, receiving guests, cleaning tables, peeling potatoes and making coffee. With just such an unstructured list, something will be left out and staff will easily become confused. It is therefore a better idea to structure the activities. Preferably these will be structured in such a way as to allow us to see how each group of activities contributes to the objectives of the business, and how they are related to other activities.

Such groups of activities are known as **processes**. If the process structure of an organization is clearly described, it will show:
• what has to be done
• what the expected inputs and results are

- how we measure whether the processes deliver the expected results
- how the results of one process affect those of another process

Processes can be defined in many ways. Depending upon the objectives of the creator, more or less emphasis will be on specific aspects. For example, a highly detailed process description will allow for a high level of control. Superficial process definitions will illustrate that the creator does not care much about the way in which the steps are executed.

Once the processes are defined, the roles, responsibilities and people can be assigned to specific aspects, bringing the process to the level of a *procedure*.

Processes

When arranging activities into processes, we do not use the existing allocation of tasks, nor the existing departmental divisions. This is a conscious choice. By opting for a process structure, it often becomes evident that certain activities in the organization are uncoordinated, duplicated, neglected or unnecessary.

> A *process* is a structured set of activities designed to accomplish a defined objective.

Instead, we look at the **objective** of the process and the **relationships** with other processes. A process is a series of activities carried out to convert input into an output, and ultimately into an outcome. The **input** is concerned with the resources being used in the process. The (reported) **output** describes the immediate results of the process, while the **outcome** indicates the long-term results of the process (in terms of meaningful effect). Through **control** activities, we can associate the input and output of each of the processes with **policies and standards** to provide information about the results to be obtained by the process. Control regulates the input and the **throughput** in case the throughput or output parameters are not compliant with these standards and policies. This produces chains of processes that show the input that goes into the organization and what the result, and it also monitors points in the chains in order to check the quality of the products and services provided by the organization.

The standards for the output of each process have to be defined, in such a way that the complete chain of processes in the process model meets the corporate objective. If the output of a process meets the defined requirements, then the process is **effective** in transforming its input into its output. To be really effective, the outcome should be taken into consideration rather than merely focusing on the output. If the activities in the process are also carried out with the minimum required effort and cost, then the process is **efficient**. It is the task of process management to use **planning and control** to ensure that processes are executed in an effective and efficient way.

We can study each process separately to optimize its quality. The **process owner** is responsible for the process results. The **process manager** is responsible for the realization and structure of the process, and reports to the process owner.

The logical combination of activities results in clear transfer points where the quality of processes can be monitored. In the restaurant example, we can separate responsibility for purchasing and cooking, so that the chefs do not have to purchase anything and can concentrate on their core activities.

The management of the organization can provide control on the basis of the process quality of the process as demonstrated by data from the results of each process. In most cases, the relevant **performance indicators** and standards will already be agreed upon. In this case the process manager can do the day-to-day control of the process. The process owner will assess the results based on a **report** of performance indicators and checks whether the results meet the agreed standard. Without clear indicators, it would be difficult for a process owner to determine whether the process is under control, and if planned improvements are being implemented.

Processes are often described using **procedures** and **work instructions**.

A **procedure** is a specified way to carry out an activity or a process. A procedure describes the "how", and can also describe "who" carries the activities out. A procedure may include stages from different processes. A procedure can vary depending on the organization.

A set of **work instructions** defines how one or more activities in a procedure should be carried out in detail, using technology or other resources.

A process is defined as a logically related series of activities executed to meet the goals of a defined objective. Processes are composed of two kinds of activities: the activities to realize the goal (operational activities concerned with the throughput), and the activities to manage these (control activities). The control activities make sure the operational activities (the workflow) are performed in time, in the right order, etc. (For example, in the processing of changes it is always ensured that a test is performed *before* a release is taken into production and not *afterwards*.)

Processes and departments

Most businesses are hierarchically organized. There are departments that are responsible for the activities of a group of employees. There are various ways of structuring departments, such as by customer, product, region or discipline. IT services generally depend on several departments, customers or disciplines. For example, if there is an IT service to provide users with access to an accounting program on a central computer, this will involve several disciplines. The computer center has to make the program and database accessible, the data and telecommunications department has to make the computer center accessible, and the PC support team has to provide users with an interface to access the application.

Processes that span several departments (teams) can monitor the quality of a service by monitoring particular aspects of quality, such as availability, capacity, cost and stability. A service organization will try to match these quality aspects with the customer's demands. The structure of such processes can ensure that good information is available about the provision of services, so that the planning and control of services can be improved.

Figure 4.1 shows a basic example of the combinations of activities in a process (indicated by the dashed lines).

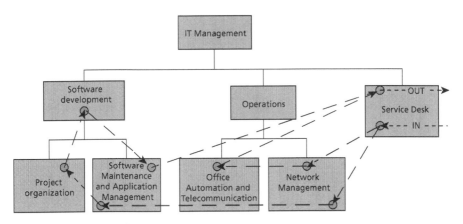

Figure 4.1 Processes and departments

IT service management and processes

IT service management has been known as the process and service-focused approach of what was initially known as Information Technology management. The shift of management from infrastructure to processes has paved the way for the term IT service management as a process and customer-focused discipline. Processes should always have a defined objective. The objective of IT service management processes is to contribute to the quality of the IT services. Quality management and process control are part of the organization and its policies.

By using a process approach, best practices for IT service management describe how services can be delivered, using the most effective and efficient series of activities. The Service Lifecycle in ITIL V3 is based on these process descriptions. The structure and allocation of tasks and responsibilities between functions and departments depends on the type of organization, and these structures vary widely among IT departments, and they often change. The description of the process structure however, provides a common point of reference that changes less rapidly. This can help to maintain the quality of IT services during and after reorganizations, and also among service providers and partners as they change. This makes service providers far less sensitive to organizational change, and much more flexible: providers can continually adapt their organization to changing conditions, leaving the core of their processes in place. In this way the shop can stay open during reconstruction work. However, reality may pose some practical problems, making this more difficult in practice than it seems in theory.

Applying the best process definitions of the industry allows IT service providers to concentrate on their business. As with other fields of industry, the processes in the IT industry are similar for all organizations of the same nature. Many of the process descriptions documented in ITIL have been recognized as the best that the industry could hope to adopt.

4.3   Teams, roles and positions in ITSM

Organizations divide the various tasks for carrying out processes or activities in many different ways. Tasks can be covered by organizational bodies, such as groups, teams, departments or divisions. These organizational bodies are then managed in **hierarchical organizations** by a line manager, who has a certain "span of control" and who manages one or more of these bodies. **Flat organizations** have relatively few layers in this hierarchy. Organizations can also divide the tasks more in the spirit of equality, such as, for example, **network organizations**, in which the cooperation between the various bodies is paramount.

Besides hierarchical organizations, which manage through "the line", there are also **project organizations**, which manage primarily by using temporary forms of project cooperation, while **process organizations** are managed primarily by means of an agreed work method. Obviously, these types of management can be combined in innumerable ways. As a result of this, we are seeing a great number of unique organizational configurations in the field.

Organizations can distinguish themselves from other organizations, particularly in respect to the type of organization they operate. An organization that is directed toward hierarchy will have a staff primarily of senior line management. A process-oriented organization will have staff that are responsible for processes. Depending on the degree to which management is based on processes, the line or projects, the staff will consist of a mix of the relevant responsible managers.

When setting up an organization, positions and roles are also used, in addition to the various groups (teams, departments, divisions). **Roles** are sets of responsibilities, activities and authorities granted to a person or team. One person or team may have multiple roles; for example, the roles of Configuration Manager and Change Manager may be carried out by a single person. **Positions** (functions) are traditionally recognized as tasks and responsibilities that are assigned to a specific person. A person in a particular position has a clearly defined package of tasks and responsibilities which may include various roles. Positions can also be more broadly defined as a logical concept that refers to the people and automated measures that carry out a clearly defined process, an activity or a combination of processes or activities.

4.4 Tools used in ITSM

In the performance of tasks in IT service management, innumerable automated support aids can be used: these are referred to as tools. With the help of these tools, management tasks can be automated; for example, monitoring tasks or software distribution tasks. Other tools support the performance of the activities themselves; for example, service desk tools or service management tools. The latter category, in fact, supports the management of several processes and are therefore often referred to as workflow tools - although they may not have actual workflow engines.

The fact that the IT field is fundamentally focused on automated facilities (for information processing) has led to a virtual deluge of tools appearing on the market, which have greatly increased the performance capacity of IT organizations.

4.5 Communication in IT service organizations

People, process, partners and technology provide the main "machinery" of any organization, but they only work well if the machine is oiled: **communication** is an essential element in any organization. If the people do not know about the processes or use the wrong instructions or tools, the output may not be as anticipated.

People are core assets of the organization. This is not only due to the fact that they need to be in place to perform certain activities or to take decisions, but also because people have the good habit of communicating. When an organization applies highly detailed instructions for all its activities, it will end up in a bureaucracy. On the other hand, an organization without any rules is will most likely end up in chaos. Whichever balance an organization is trying to find here, it will always benefit enormously from communication between the people in the organization. A regular and formal meeting culture will support this, but organizations should not underestimate the important role of informal communication: many projects have been saved by means of a simple chat in the tea room, or in the car park.

Formal structures on communication include:
- **reporting** - internal and external reporting, aimed at management or customers, project progress reports, alerts
- **meetings** - formal project meetings, regular meetings with specific targets
- **online facilities** - email systems, chat-rooms, pagers, groupware, document sharing systems, messenger facilities, teleconferencing and virtual meeting facilities
- **notice boards** - near the coffee maker, water cooler, at the entrance of the building, in the company restaurant

IT teams and departments, as well as users, internal customers and service production teams, must communicate with each other. The **stakeholders** for communication can thus be found among all managers and employees who are involved in service management, in all the layers of the organization, and with all customers, users and service providers. Good communication can prevent problems. All communication must have a particular goal or result. Every team, process and every department must have a clear **communications policy**.

IT service management includes several types of communication, such as:
- routine operational communication
- communication between teams
- performance reports
- communication during projects

- communication when there are changes
- communication in case of exceptions
- communication in case of emergencies
- training for new or adapted processes and service designs
- communication with service production teams regarding service strategies and design

4.6 Culture

Organizations that want to change, for example to improve the quality of their services, will eventually be confronted with the current organizational culture and will have to deal with any changes to this culture as a consequence of the overall change. The organizational culture, or corporate culture, refers to the way in which people deal with each other in the organization; the way in which decisions are made and implemented; and the attitude of employees to their work, customers, service providers, superiors and colleagues.

Culture, which depends on the standards and values of the people in the organization, cannot be controlled, but it can be influenced. Influencing the culture of an organization requires leadership in the form of a clear and consistent policy, as well as a supportive personnel policy.

The corporate culture can have a major influence on the provision of IT services. Businesses value innovation in different ways. In a stable organization, where the culture places little value on innovation, it will be difficult to adjust its IT services in line with changes in the organization of the customer. If the IT department is unstable, then a culture which values change can pose a serious threat to the quality of its services. In that case, a "free for all" culture can develop where many uncontrolled changes lead to a large number of faults.

4.7 Processes, projects, programs and portfolios

Activities can be managed from a process perspective, from an organizational hierarchy (line) perspective, from a project perspective, or from any combination of these three. Organizations that tend to apply just one of these management systems often miss the benefits of the others. The practical choice often depends upon history, culture, available skills and competences, and personal preferences. The optimum choice may be entirely different, but the requirements for applying this optimum may be hard to realize and vary in time.

There are no "hard and fast laws" for the way an organization should combine processes, projects and programs. However, it is generally accepted that there are some consequences attached to modern practices in IT service organizations, since the most widely accepted approach to service management is based on process management. This means that whenever the organization works with projects or programs, it should have established how these approaches work together.

The practical relationship between projects and processes is determined by the relative position of both in terms of "leading principles for the management of the organization": if projects are considered more important than processes, then decisions on projects will overrule decisions on processes; as a consequence, the organization will not be able to implement a stable set of processes. If it is the other way around, with projects only able to run within the constraints of agreed processes, then project management will be a discipline that will have to adapt to new boundaries and definitions (e.g. since projects always change something from A to B, they will most likely fall under the regime of Change, Release and Deployment Management).

The most suitable solution is dependent upon the understanding of the role of IT service management in the organization. To be able to find a solution for this management challenge, it is recommended that a common understanding of processes, projects, programs, and even portfolio's is created. The following definitions may be used:
- **Process** - A process is a structured set of activities designed to accomplish a defined objective.
- **Project** - A project is a temporary organization, with people and other assets required to achieve an objective.
- **Program** - A program consists of a number of projects and activities that are planned and managed together to achieve an overall set of related objectives.
- **Portfolio** - A portfolio is a set of projects and/or programs, which are not necessarily related, brought together for the sake of control, coordination and optimization of the portfolio in its totality. NB: In ITIL, a service portfolio is the complete set of services that are managed by a service provider.

Since the project/program/portfolio grouping is a hierarchical set of essential project resources, the issue can be downscaled to that of a relationship between a project and a process.

The most elementary difference between a process and a project is the one-off character of a project, versus the continuous character of the process. If a project has achieved its objectives, it means the end of the project. Processes can be run many times, both in parallel and in sequence. The nature of a process is aimed at its repeatable character:

processes are defined only in case of a repeatable string of activities that are important enough to be standardized and optimized.

Projects are aimed at changing a situation A into a situation B. This can involve a simple string of activities, but it can also be a very complex series of activities. Other elements of importance for projects include money, time, quality, organization and information. Project structures are normally used only if at least one of these elements is of considerable value.

Actually, projects are just ways of organizing a specific change in a situation. In that respect they have a resemblance with processes. It is often a matter of focus: processes focus at the specific sequence of activities, the decisions taken at certain milestone stages, and the quality of the activities involved. Processes are continuously instantiated and repeated, and use the same approach each time. Projects focus more at the time and money constraints, in terms of resources spent on the change and the projects end, and projects vary much more than processes.

A very practical way of combining the benefits of both management systems might be as follows:

- Processes set the scene for how specific series of activities are performed.
- Projects can be used to transform situation A into situation B, and always refer to a change.
- If the resources (time, money, or other) involved in a specific process require the level of attention that is normally applied in a project, then (part of) the process activities can be performed as a project, but always under the control of the process: if changes are performed, using project management techniques, the agreed change management policies still apply.

This would allow organizations to maintain a continuous customer focus and apply a process approach to optimize this customer focus, and at the same time benefit from the high level of resource control that can be achieved when using project management techniques.

4.8 Functions and processes in the lifecycle phases

For the sake of readability and uniformity, the following structure for the descriptions was used as much as possible:

- **introduction** - describes the purpose and aims of the process or function, its scope, value to the business, principles, guidelines, starting points and basic concepts

- **activities, methods and techniques** - explains the process or function in greater detail based on the workflow of activities (if possible); also describes commonly used methods and techniques
- **interfaces** - describes how the process or function is triggered, its inputs and outputs, and its links to other functions and processes
- **metrics** - describes the process metrics, in particular the Key Performance Indicators (KPIs)
- **implementation** - describes the Critical Success Factors (CSFs), challenges, risks and traps that may apply for the introduction of a process or function

CHAPTER 5

Functions and Processes in Service Design

5.1 Service Catalogue Management

Introduction

The **purpose** of Service Catalogue Management (SCM) is to provide a single source of consistent information on all of the agreed services, and ensure that it is widely available to those who are approved to access it.

The **goal** of service catalogue management is the development and upkeep of a service catalogue that contains all accurate details, the status, possible interactions and mutual dependencies of all current services and those being prepared to run operationally.

Value for the business

The service catalogue is the central resource of information on the IT services delivered by the service provider organization. This ensures that all areas of the business can view an accurate, consistent picture of the IT services, their details and their status. It contains a customer facing view of the IT services in use, how they are intended to be used, the business processes they enable, and the level of quality of service the customer can expect for each service.

Basic concepts

Over the years, the IT infrastructures of organizations grow at a rapid pace and there may not be a clear picture of the services offered by the organizations and whom they are offered to. To get a clearer picture, a service portfolio is developed (with a service catalogue as part of it), and maintained. The development of the service portfolio is a component of the Service Strategy phase. The Portfolio needs subsequent support from the other phases in the lifecycle.

It is important to make a clear distinction between the portfolio and the catalogue:

- **Service portfolio** - The portfolio contains information about each service and its status. As a result, the Portfolio describes the entire process, starting with the client requirements for the development, building and execution of the service. The service portfolio represents all active and inactive services in the various phases of the lifecycle.
- **Service catalogue** - The catalogue is a subset of the service portfolio and consists only of active and approved services (at retail level) in Service Operation. The catalogue divides services into components. It contains policies, guidelines and responsibilities, as well as prices, service level arrangements and delivery conditions. The client gets to review the largest part of the service catalogue.

Many organizations integrate and maintain the portfolio and catalogue as a part of their Configuration Management System (CMS). By defining every service, a Configuration Item (CI) must be defined and, when possible, incorporated into a hierarchy, the organization can relate the incidents and requests for change to the services in question. It is for this reason that changes in both portfolio and catalogue must be part of the change management process.

The service catalogue can also be used for a Business Impact Analysis (BIA) as part of IT Service Continuity Management (ITSCM), or as starting point for the re-distribution of the workload as part of the capacity management. These benefits justify the investment (in time and money) involved in preparing a Catalogue and making it worthwhile.

The service catalogue has two aspects:

- **The business service catalogue** contains details of the services that are being supplied to the customer together with the relationships to the business units and the business processes that rely on the IT services. This is the customer view of the service catalogue. The business service catalogue facilitates the development of proactive and preemptive SLM processes, allowing it to develop more into the field of Business Service Management (BSM).
- **The technical service catalogue** contains details of the IT services supplied to the customer, together with relationships to the supporting and shared services, components and CIs. This is the part that is not visible to the client. The technical

service catalogue explains which technical aspects (and departments) are necessary to render the service.

A combination of both catalogues provides a quick overview on the impact of incidents and changes on the business. For this reason, many mature organizations combine both aspects in a service catalogue, as part of a service portfolio.

Activities, methods and techniques

The service catalogue is the only resource which contains constant information about all services of the service provider. The catalogue should be accessible to every authorized person. Activities in this process include:

* agreeing and documenting a service definition with all relevant parties
* interfacing with service portfolio management to agree the contents of the service portfolio and service catalogue
* producing and maintaining an accurate service catalogue and its contents in conjunction with the service portfolio
* interfacing with the business and IT service continuity management on the dependencies of business units and their business processes with the supporting IT services, contained within the business service catalogue
* interfacing with support teams, service providers and configuration management on interfaces and dependencies between IT services and the supporting services, components and CIs contained within the technical service catalogue
* interfacing with business relationship management and service level management to ensure that the information is aligned to the business and business process

Interfaces

Inputs are:

* business information from the organization's business and IT strategy, plans and financial plans etc.
* business impact analysis
* service portfolio
* CMS
* Feedback from other processes

Outputs are:

* documentation and agreement of a "definition of the service"
* updates to the service portfolio
* updated to the service catalogue

Metrics

KPIs are:

- the number of services recorded and maintained within the service catalogue as a percentage of those being delivered and transitioned in the live environment
- the number of differences discovered between the information from the service catalogue and reality
- percentage increase in the completeness of the business service catalogue, compared with the operational services
- percentage increase in the completeness of the technical service catalogue, compared with the IT components in support of the services
- access of the service desk to information in support of the services, expressed by the percentage of incidents without the appropriate service-related information

Implementation

The most important challenge in the service catalogue management process is maintaining an accurate service catalogue (containing both the Business and the Technical aspect) as part of the service portfolio. In order to achieve this, spreadsheets or databases must be developed before integrating the service catalogue or service portfolio into the Configuration Management System (CMS) and Service Knowledge Management System (SKMS). In addition, it is important that all parties involved recognize that both catalogues are essential sources of information which must be used and maintained by everyone in the IT organization.

Critical success factors are:

- accurate service catalogue
- business users' awareness of the services being provided
- IT staff awareness of the technology supporting the services

Risks include:

- inaccurate information in the catalogue and it not being under change management control
- poor acceptance of the service catalogue and its use in the operational processes
- inaccuracy of the information supplied by the business, IT and service portfolio
- tools and resources needed to keep the information up-to-date
- poor access to accurate change management information and processes
- circumvention of the use of the service portfolio and service catalogue
- information too detailed to maintain accurately or at too high level to be of any value

5.2 Service Level Management

Introduction

The **goal** of the Service Level Management (SLM) process is to ensure that an agreed level of IT service is provided for all current IT services, and that future services are delivered to agreed achievable targets.

The **objectives** are:
- defining, documenting, agreeing, monitoring, measuring, reporting and executing a review of the service level
- delivering and improving the relation and communication with the business and the clients
- ensuring that specific and measurable targets are being developed
- monitoring and improving customer satisfaction with the quality of service being delivered
- ensuring that the IT and the customers have a clear and unambiguous expectation of the level of service to be delivered
- ensuring that proactive measures to improve levels of service delivered are implemented wherever it is cost-justifiable to do so

Scope

SLM represents the IT service provider client the business, and the business to the IT service provider. There is regular bi-directional contact, whereby both the present service and the future service are discussed. SLM has to manage the expectations of both parties (both internal and external). In addition, SLM assures the quality of service delivered meets the expectations.

The SLM process should include the following items:
- development of business relationships
- development and management of Operational Level Agreements (OLAs)
- reviewing underpinning supplier contracts
- proactive prevention of service failures, reduction of service risks and improvement in service quality
- reporting and managing all services and review of SLA breaches and weaknesses

Value for the business

SLM provides a consistent interface to the business for all service related issues. It provides the business with the agreed service targets and the required management information to ensure that those targets have been met. Where targets are breached, SLM should provide feedback on the cause of the breach and details of the actions being taken to prevent the breach recurring.

The service level management process entails planning, coordinating, drafting, agreeing, monitoring and reporting on Service Level Agreements (SLAs), and the ongoing review of service achievements to ensure that the required and cost-justifiable service quality is maintained and gradually improved. The SLA is a written agreement between the Service Provider and its customers defining service targets and responsibilities of both parties.

On the other hand, an OLA is an agreement between an IT service provider and another part of the same organization that assists with the provision of services.

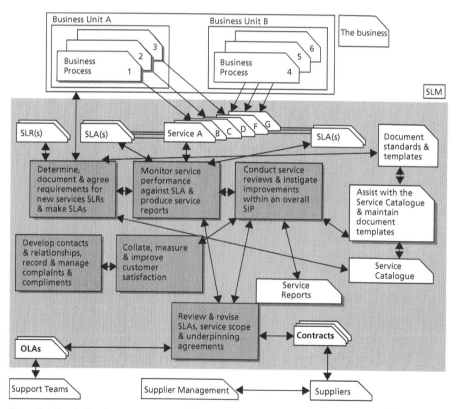

Figure 5.1 Service level management process

Activities, methods and techniques

The activities of service level management (Figure 5.1) are:

- **Design of SLA Frameworks** - SLM has to design the most appropriate SLA structure, so that all services and all customers are covered in a manner best suited to organizational needs. There are a number of options including the following:
    - **service-based SLAs** - an SLA covers one service for all customers of that service; an SLA can be established for e-mail services or for supplying certain telephone facilities, for example. This framework can cause difficulties if the specific requirements of one customer vary for the same service.
    - **customer-based SLAs** - an agreement with a customer containing all services they use; the customer often prefers this SLA because all of their requirements are captured in one single document
    - **multi-level SLAs** - a combination having for example the following structure:
        - corporate level, covering all generic SLM matters
        - customer level, covering all SLM issues which are relevant to a specific group of customers or business units
        - service level, covering all subjects that are relevant to a specific service relating to a specific customer

      The multi-level SLA keeps the SLAs to a manageable size and reduces the need for frequent updates.
- **Determining, documenting and agreeing on the requirements for new services and production of Service Level Requirements (SLRs)** - Once the service catalogue is produced and the SLA structure determined, the first SLR needs to be drafted; at this stage, both customer and the other departments should be involved, in order to prevent the situation where the customer is faced with a "fait accompli" at a later stage and in order to find out how realistic the arrangements are.
- **Monitoring the performance with regard to the SLA and reporting the outcome** - Everything that is incorporated into the SLA must be measurable; otherwise disputes may arise, which may eventually result in confidence loss of faith; for example, the service provider can measure incident response time; report regularly regarding the results and use these reports for discussion with the customer; it is also recommended that all complaints and compliments are recorded and then discussed these with the relevant parties.
- **Improving customer satisfaction** - Besides the "hard" monitoring listed, customer satisfaction with the service provision should be taken into account; this can be done by using questionnaires, for example.
- **Review and revise underpinning agreements** - The IT service provider is dependent to some extent on their own internal technical services (or external partners and suppliers); in order to meet the SLA targets, the underpinning agreements with

internal departments (OLAs) must support the SLA as must the contracts with external parties; the agreements must at all times be up-to-date and incorporated into the change management and configuration management processes.

- **Produce service reports** - Communication is a core activity in service management and requires adequate reporting. Reporting mechanisms should be specified and agreed, and reports should be delivered at regular intervals. Service reports are input to service review meetings. The reports should contain accurate information from all areas and processes that is integrated into a comprehensive report on service performance, measured against agreed business targets.

- **Reviewing and improving services** - Consult regularly with the customer to evaluate the services and identify possible improvements in the service provision; focus on those improvement items that yield the greatest benefit to the business; report regularly on the progress of the improvements and incorporate them in the Service Improvement Plan (SIP).

- **Review and revise SLAs** - All agreements should be subject to change and configuration management and reviewed periodically, to make sure that changes to the service infrastructure haven't invalidated the agreements.

- **Developing contacts and relations** - SLM has to instill confidence in the business; by using the service catalogue, SLM can start working proactively; the catalogue supplies information with which the relation between services and the business units and the business processes which are dependent on these services, can be better understood; in order to do this thoroughly, SLM can carry out the following activities among others:
    - consulting and informing stakeholders, customers and managers
    - maintaining accurate information in the service portfolio and service catalogue
    - adopting a flexible and responsive attitude towards customer needs
    - developing a full understanding of the business and customer
    - undertake customer satisfaction surveys

With regard to *information management*:
- supplies crucial information to SLM regarding operational services, goals set and "infractions"
- supports SLM service catalogue management by means of the service catalogue
- supplies information and trends to SLM concerning customer satisfaction

Interfaces
Inputs are:
- business information arising from the organization's business strategy, plans and financial plans
- business requirements
- service portfolio and service catalogue
- change information
- Configuration Management System (CMS)

Outputs are:
- service reports
- Service Improvement Plan (SIP)
- Service Quality Plan (SQP)
- standard document templates
- SLA, SLR and OLAs
- Service review meeting minutes

Metrics
KPIs include:
- percentage reduction in SLA targets missed
- percentage increase in customer satisfaction
- percentage reduction in SLA breaches

Implementation
Possible **triggers** for SLM activity are:
- changes in service portfolio
- new or modified agreements
- changes in strategy or policy
- compliments and complaints
- service review meetings and actions

5.3   Capacity Management

Introduction

The **goal** of capacity management is to ensure that cost-justifiable IT capacity in all areas of IT always exists and is matched to the current and future agreed needs of the business in timely manner.

Capacity management is supported initially in Service Strategy where the decisions and analysis of business requirements and customer outcomes influence the development of Patterns of Business Activity (PBA), Lines of Service (LOS) and Service Level Packages (SLPs). This provides the predictive and ongoing capacity indicators needs to align capacity to demand.

The **objectives** of capacity management are:
*   creating and maintaining an up-to-date capacity plan that reflects the current and future needs of the customer
*   internal and external consulting on services in terms of capacity and performance
*   ensuring that the services provided comply with the defined objectives by managing both the performance and the capacity of services
*   contributing to diagnosis of performance and capacity-related incidents and problems
*   investigating the impact of all changes to the capacity plan
*   taking proactive measures to improve performance

Scope

The capacity management process should be the focal point for all IT performance and capacity issues. Network and server support or operation management may take on the majority of day-to-day operational duties, but will provide performance information to the capacity management process. In addition, capacity management also considers space planning and environmental systems capacity. It may also have a task in certain human resource aspects but only where a lack of human resources could result in a breach of OLA or SLA. However, Human Resource Management (HRM) is the main responsibility of line management though the staffing of a service desk could use identical capacity management techniques.

The drivers behind this process are the customer requirements as laid down in the SLA. Because capacity management understands the total IT and customer environment, it is able to comply with current *and* future capacity and performance requirements in a cost-effective manner. Managing large IT infrastructures is a difficult and demanding task, in particular if the IT capacity and required financial investments are growing. Planning is vital to realize economies of scale, for instance, when buying components.

Capacity management should have input to the service portfolio and procurement process to ensure that the best deals with IT service providers are negotiated. Capacity management provides the necessary information on current and planned resource utilization of individual components to enable organizations to decide with confidence:
- which components to upgrade
- when to upgrade
- how much the upgrade will cost

Capacity management has a close two-way relationship with Service Strategy since the latter is based on the organization plans, which in turn are derived from the strategy. In other words, it must understand the short, medium and long-term plans of the organization in order to function properly.

Other processes are less effective as well if they do not receive input from capacity management. For example what is the effect of a change (change management) on the available capacity or are the agreed service level requirements of a new service achievable (SLM). Thorough capacity management is able to predict events (and their impact) before they occur.

Value for the business
Capacity management is responsible for planning and scheduling IT resources to provide a consistent service level that matches the current and future requirements of the customer. Capacity management delivers a capacity plan in consultation with the customer. The plan specifies the IT and financial resources that are necessary to support the business, including a cost justification of expenditure.

The capacity management process involves balancing cost against resources needed and balancing supply against demand.

Capacity management processes and planning must be involved in every phase of the Service Lifecycle, from strategy and design through Transition and Operation to Continual Service Improvement.

Activities, methods and techniques

The capacity management process (Figure 5.2) consists of:

- **reactive activities**, such as:
  - monitoring
  - measuring
- **proactive activities**, such as:
  - predicting future requirements
  - producing trends

The more proactive the capacity management process, the lesser the need for reactive activities.

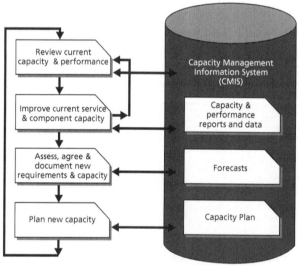

Figure 5.2 The capacity management process

Capacity management is an extremely technical, complex and demanding process that comprises three sub-processes (Figure 5.2):

- **Business Capacity Management (BCM)** - Translates the customer's requirements to specifications for the service and IT infrastructure; it focuses on current and future requirements; involve business capacity management in:
  - **support** - when establishing Service Level Requirements (SLRs), capacity management must support SLM in understanding the requirements defined by the customer for capacity and performance

- **designing and changing service configurations** - capacity management must be involved in the development of new and modified services and make recommendations for purchasing hardware and software if performance and capacity factors have an impact
- **verifying the SLA** - capacity management advises SLM on achievable targets that can be measured
- **approving the SLA** - providing support to SLM if new negotiations are necessary by mapping possible solutions and related costs
- **controlling and implementing** - all changes to service and resource capacity must follow all IT processes such as change, release, configuration and project management to ensure that the right degree of control and coordination is in place on all changes and that any new or changed components are recorded and tracked through their lifecycle
- **Service capacity management** - The main purpose of this sub-process is to identify and understand the IT services (including the resources, working patterns, peaks and troughs etc.) and to ensure that the services meet their SLA targets; service capacity management monitors services, measures their performance, records the data, analyzes the data, and reports on this information; this sub-process focuses on managing, controlling and predicting the performance and capacity of (existing) operational IT services.
- **Component Capacity Management (CCM)** - This sub-process focuses primarily on managing, controlling and predicting the performance, use and capacity of individual IT components, such as processors, network and bandwidth; the emphasis is on IT infrastructure that supports the services; this is primarily an activity executed in the Service Operation phase.

Supporting activities of capacity management
Some activities must be executed repeatedly (proactively or reactively) (Figure 5.3). They provide basic information and triggers for other activities and processes in capacity management. These activities include:

- tuning and optimization
- utilization monitoring
- response time monitoring
- analysis
- implementation
- exploitation of new technology
- designing resilience

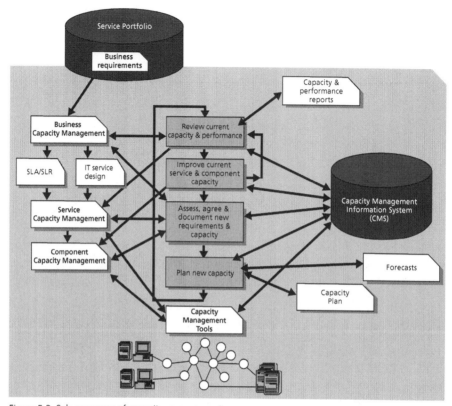

Figure 5.3 Sub-processes of capacity management

Capacity management also includes:
- threshold management and control
- demand management
- predicting "the behavior" of IT services by using modeling methods such as:
  - baseline model
  - trend analysis
  - analytical model
  - simulation model
- application sizing, estimating the requirements for resources to support proposed changes

Information management and the capacity management information system
The aim of the Capacity Management Information System (CMIS) is to provide relevant information on the capacity and performance of services and infrastructure in order

to support the capacity management process. This information system is one of the most important elements in the capacity management process. All of the capacity management sub-processes analyze the information stored. For instance, it contains business information on the current and future needs of the customer. It also contains data on services, such as response times, information on component usage (e.g. server traffic), and financial data (such as the costs involved in updates).

Interfaces

Capacity management activities can be **triggered** by, among other things, disruptions in services, capacity and performance warnings, new and changed services, changes to business and IT plans and strategies and the review and revision of SLAs, OLAs, contracts or any other agreement.

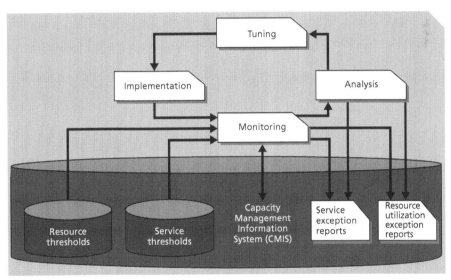

Figure 5.4 Iterative activities in capacity management

Input

- business information from the organizations business strategy, plans and financial plans, and information on their current and future requirements
- service and IT information from IT strategy and plans
- component performance and capacity information
- service performance issues from incident and problem management
- financial information

- change and performance information
- CMIS
- Workload information from Operations team

Output
- Capacity Management Information System (CMIS)
- Capacity plan with information on current usage of services and components as well as plans to meet the growth in services and new services
- service performance information and reports
- workload analysis and reports
- forecasts and predictive reports
- thresholds, alerts and events

Metrics
To evaluate efficiency and effectiveness activities should include:
- percentage accuracy of forecasts of business trends
- production of workload forecasts on time
- increased ability to monitor performance and throughput of services and components
- timely justification and implementation of new technology
- reduction in use of old technology
- reduction in Incidents and Problems related to inadequate capacity

Implementation
One of the main **challenges** is to convince the customer to supply more strategic information. This enables the service provider to ensure effective business continuity management. This can be particularly important when services are provided via outsourcing. Another challenge is to integrate the component capacity management (CCM) information so that it can be analyzed in a consistent manner. As a result, capacity management is able to supply detailed information on component usage.

Critical success factors include:
- accuracy of business predictions
- knowledge of current and future technologies
- ability to demonstrate cost effectiveness
- ability to plan and implement the appropriate IT capacity to meet business needs

The **risks** include:
- lack of commitment from the business
- lack of accurate information on the strategy and organization plans
- the creation of bureaucratic or manually intensive processes

5.4 Availability Management

Introduction

The **goal** of availability management is to ensure that the level of service availability delivered in all services is matched to or exceeds the current and future agreed needs of the business, in a cost effective manner.

Its **objectives** are:
- creating and maintaining an up-to-date availability plan that reflects the current and future needs of the customer
- advising on availability-related issues
- guiding the customer and IT service provider
- ensuring that availability results meet or exceed the defined requirements
- providing assistance in diagnosis and resolution of availability-related incidents and problems
- assessing the impact of changes have on the availability plan and the performance and capacity of the services and resources
- taking proactive measures to improve availability

Scope

Availability management includes designing, implementing, measuring, managing and improving IT services and the components availability. It must understand the service and component availability requirements from the business perspective in terms of the:
- current business processes (their operation and requirements)
- future business plans and requirements
- service targets and the current Service Operation and delivery
- IT infrastructure, data, applications and the environment (including performance)
- business impacts and priorities n relation to the services and their usage

By understanding these issues, availability management is able to ensure that all services and components are designed and delivered in order to meet their targets in terms of agreed business need. Availability management should be applied to all operational services, new, modified and supporting services. It covers all service aspects that have an impact on availability, such as training, competencies, procedures and tools.

Value for the business

The availability and reliability of IT services has a direct impact on customer satisfaction and company reputation. As such, availability management is vital. It should therefore be included (just like capacity management) in all stages of the Service Lifecycle.

Activities, methods and techniques

The main activities of availability management are (Figure 5.5):

- determining the availability requirements of the business
- determining the Vital Business Functions (VBFs)
- determining the impact of failing components
- defining the targets for availability, reliability and maintainability of the IT components
- monitoring and analyzing IT components
- establishing measures and reporting of availability, reliability, and maintainability that reflect the business user and IT support organization perspectives
- investigating the underlying reasons for unacceptable availability
- creating and maintaining an availability plan

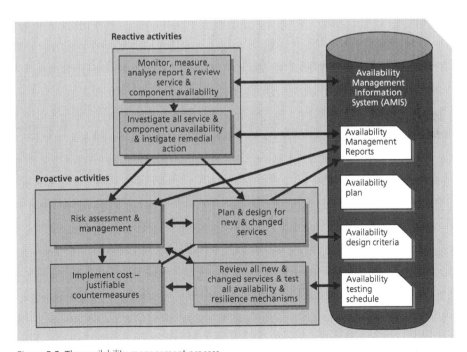

Figure 5.5 The availability management process

Availability management monitors, measures, analyzes and reports on the following aspects:

- **availability** - the service, component or CIs ability to perform its agreed function when required
- **reliability** - the length of time a service, component or CI can perform its agreed function without interruption
- **maintainability** - how quickly and effectively a service, component or CI can be restored to normal working after a failure
- **serviceability** - the ability of an external IT service provider to meet the terms of their contract

Measuring is extremely important. It can be done from three perspectives:

- **business perspective** - looks at IT availability in terms of its contribution to or impact on the Vital Business Functions that drive the business operation
- **user perspective** - views the availability of IT services as a combination of three factors: frequency, duration and scope of impact (how many users or organization parts are affected), and also response times
- **the IT service provider's perspective** - considers IT service and component availability in regard to availability, reliability and maintainability

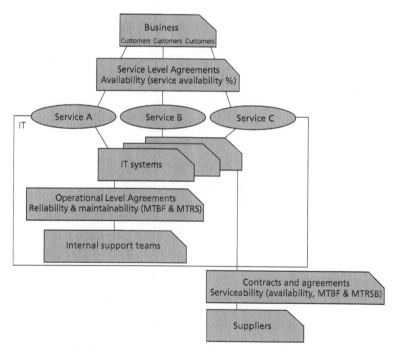

Figure 5.6 Availability terms and measurements

Availability management must ensure that all services meet their agreed targets. New or changed services must be designed in such a way that they will meet their agreed targets. To achieve this, availability management can perform reactive and proactive activities:

- **reactive activities** - are executed in the operational phase of the lifecycle:
    - monitoring, measuring, analyzing and reporting the availability of services and components
    - unavailability analysis
    - the expanded incident lifecycle
    - Service Failure Analysis (SFA)
- **proactive activities** - must be executed in the design phase of the lifecycle:
    - identifying Vital Business Functions
    - designing for availability
    - Component Failure Impact Analysis (CFIA)
    - Single Point of Failure (SPOF) analysis
    - Fault Tree Analysis (FTA)
    - modeling
    - risk analysis and management
    - availability testing schedule
    - planned and preventive maintenance
    - production of the Projected Service Availability (PSA) document
    - continual review and improvement

Leading principles

Effective availability management consists of both reactive and proactive activities. Do not lose sight of the following things:

- The availability of services is one of the most important aspects to satisfy customers.
- In the event of failures, an effective response can still result in high customer satisfaction.
- Improving availability is possibly only by understanding how the services support the customer's operations.
- Availability can only be managed as well as the weakest link in the chain.
- It is not just a reactive process, but also - and particularly - proactive.
- It is wiser and more cost-effective to build in the right availability level from the start, i.e. in the design of new services.

Starting points for availability management

Figure 5.7 illustrates a number of starting points for availability management. The unavailability of services can be reduced by aiming to reduce each of the phases distinguished in the extended incident lifecycle.

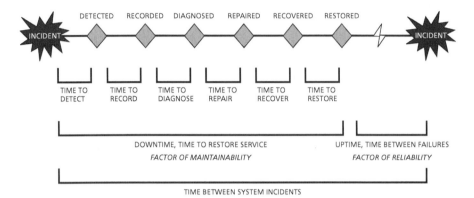

Figure 5.7 The extended incident lifecycle (Note: combination of figures from Service Strategy and Continual Service Improvement)

Services must be restored quickly when they are unavailable to users. The **Mean Time to Restore Service (MTRS)** is the time within which a function (service, system or component) is restored to operational use after a failure. The MTRS depends on a number of factors, such as:

- configuration of service assets
- MTRS of individual components
- competencies of support personnel
- available resources
- policy plans
- procedures
- redundancy

Analysis of the MTRS in relation to each factor is useful to improve the performance and design of services.

The MTRS can be reduced through management for each of its composite components (Figure 5.7). Reducing the duration of the following factors limits the unavailability time of a service:

- **incident detection** - the time between occurrence of an incident and its being detected
- **incident diagnosis** - the time at which diagnosis to determine the underlying cause has been completed
- **incident repair** - the time at which the failure has been repaired/fixed
- **incident recovery** - the time at which component recovery has been completed
- **incident restoration** - the time at which normal business service is resumed

Other metrics for measuring availability include:

- **Mean Time Between Failures (MTBF)** - The average time that a CI or service can perform its agreed function without interruption.
- **Mean Time Between Service Incidents (MTBSI)** - The mean time from when a system or service fails, until it next fails.
- **Mean Time To Repair (MTTR)** - The average time taken to repair a CI or service after a failure. MTTR is measured from when the CI or service fails until it is repaired. MTTR does not include the time required to recover or restore.

Redundancy

Redundancy is a way of increasing reliability and sustainability of systems. ITIL defines the following redundancy types:

- **Active redundancy** - This type is used to support essential services that absolutely cannot be interrupted. The productive capacity of redundancy assets is always available. With active redundancy all redundant units are operating simultaneously. For example mirrored disks in a server computer.
- **Passive redundancy** - The use of redundant assets that are left inoperative until the event of a failure (reactive). For example stand-by servers or clustered systems.

ITIL also uses the following differentiation to explain redundancy types:

- **Diverse redundancy (heterogeneous redundancy)** - Redundancy through various types of service assets that share the same capabilities (spreading the risk). This type is used when the cause of the failure is difficult to predict. For example, use of different storage media, programming languages, or development teams.
- **Homogeneous redundancy** - Refers to using extra capacity of the same type of service assets. With this type there is a high certainty about the causes of failure. For example use of two identical processors.

The active and passive redundancy types can be used individually or in combination with the homogeneous and heterogeneous types. For example: redundancy that is both active and homogeneous has a low tolerance of failure and a high certainty about the causes of failure.

The following approaches improve the accessibility of services:
- **various channels** - the demand is led through various types of access channel; this means it is resistant to the failure of a single channel (active diverse redundancy)
- **closed network** - multiple access gates increase the network's capacity (homogeneous redundancy)
- **loose link** - interfaces are based on public infrastructure, open source technologies and omnipresent access options, such as mobile phones and browsers; it offers users access to the service via multiple channels and in multiple sites; security developments are making this method increasingly accessible

Information management and the availability management information system
Availability management must maintain an information system. The Availability Management Information System (AMIS) contains all of the measures and information required to complete the availability management process. It also provides the business with the right information on the level of the service to be delivered in terms of components and supporting services.

The information system constitutes the basis for the availability plan. The availability plan is not the same as an availability management implementation plan, while it can initially be developed jointly with the implementation plan. Availability management changes all the time, which is why the availability plan must contain the following elements:
- current levels of availability compared against the agreed levels (from the customer's perspective)
- actions taken to resolve shortcomings in availability
- details of changed availability requirements for existing and future services
- a forward looking schedule for Service Failure Analysis (SFA) assignments
- regular review of the SFA assignments
- benefits and opportunities of planned upgrades

The plan should complement the capacity plan and the financial plan and cover a period of two years. The first six months should be covered in more detail. The plan should be updated with minor revisions every quarter, and major revisions occurring every six months.

Interfaces

Activities in the field of availability management are **triggered** by, among other things:
- new or changing customer needs
- new objectives in agreements e.g. SLAs, OLAs or contracts
- service failures
- availability events and alerts

Relationships with other functions and processes are:
- Availability management supports **incident and problem management** to resolve availability incidents and problems.
- Availability management provides **capacity management** with resilience and spare capacity.
- Availability management provides **IT Service Continuity Management (ITSCM)** with assessment on the impact and risks for the business and of restore mechanisms.
- Availability management assists **SLM** in determining the availability objectives and studies, and makes improvement proposals in the event of service and component failures.

The **input** of availability management is:
- business information, such as organization strategies, (financial) plans and information on the current and future requirements of IT services
- risk analyses, business impact analyses and studies of Vital Business Functions
- service information from the service portfolio and service catalogue and from the SLM process
- change calendars and release schedules from change management and release management
- service targets
- unavailability and failure information

The **output** of availability management is:
- the Availability Management Information System (AMIS)
- the availability plan
- availability and recovery design criteria
- reports on the availability, reliability and maintainability of services
- updated risk register
- monitoring, management and reporting
- availability management test schedule
- planned and preventive maintenance schedule
- Projected Service Outage (PSO)

Metrics

Organizations can use various **KPIs** to measure the effectiveness and efficiency of availability management, such as:

- percentage reduction in the unavailability of services and components
- percentage increase in the of reliability of services and components
- percentage improvement in overall end-to-end availability of service
- percentage reduction of the cost of unavailability
- percentage increase in customer satisfaction

Implementation

Availability management has the following **challenges**:

- meeting the expectations of customers, the business and the management
- integrating all availability information into an availability management information system
- convincing the business and management of the need to invest in proactive availability measures

Critical success factors for availability management are:

- managing the availability and reliability of IT services
- availability of IT infrastructure (as agreed in the SLAs) provided at optimal costs
- satisfying business needs for access to IT services

Risks for availability management are:

- lack of commitment from the business to the availability management process
- lack of adequate information on plans and strategies for the future
- lack of resources and funds
- increasing labor-intensive reporting

5.5   IT Service Continuity Management

Introduction

The **goal** of IT Service Continuity Management (ITSCM) is to support the overall business continuity process by ensuring that the required IT technical and service facilities (including computer systems, networks, applications, data repositories, telecommunications, environment, technical support and service desk etc.) can be resumed within required and agreed business timescales.

Objectives include:
- maintaining a set of continuity plans and recovery plans
- performing regular Business Impact Analysis (BIA)
- conducting regular risk estimates and management exercises
- provide advice and guidance to all other areas of the business and IT on all continuity and recovery-related issues
- ensuring that the appropriate continuity and recovery mechanisms are put in place to meet or exceed the agreed business continuity targets
- assessing the impact of all changes on the continuity and recovery plans
- implementing proactive measures to improve the availability of services (where cost-justifiable to do so)
- negotiating agreements with IT service providers in relation to the required recovery capability to support continuity plans

Scope

ITSCM focuses on those events that the business considers a disaster. The incident management process handles less significant events. ITSCM primarily considers the IT assets and configurations that support the business processes. If it is necessary to move to an alternative work environment as a result of a disaster, the process also covers office spaces, personnel accommodation and telephone facilities, for example.

ITSCM does not usually directly cover longer-term risks such as those from changes in business direction. While these can have a huge impact, there is generally enough time to identify them and take action. Minor technical problems, such as non critical disk failures, are not covered by this process - they are handled by incident management. ITSCM does cover:
- agreements on ITSCM's scope
- a business impact analysis to quantify the impact of disasters
- Risk Analysis (RA) - risk identification and risk assessment to identify potential threats to continuity and the likelihood of the threats becoming reality

- creating an overall ITSCM strategy that must be integrated into the business continuity management strategy
- creating continuity plans
- testing the plans
- ongoing operation and maintenance of the plans

Value for the business

ITSCM has a valuable role in supporting the business continuity planning process. Organizations often use it to create awareness of continuity and recovery requirements and justify their decision to implement the process of business continuity planning (including plans).

Activities, methods and techniques

ITSCM is a cyclic process. It keeps the developed service continuity plans and recovery plans in line with the business continuity plans as these are updated.

The process consists of four phases (Figure 5.8):
1. **Initiation** - This phase covers the entire organization and includes the following activities:
   - defining the policy
   - specifying terms of reference and scope
   - allocating resources (people, resources and funds)
   - defining the project organization and control structure
   - agree project and quality plans
2. **Requirements and strategy** - Determining the business requirements for ITSCM is vital when investigating how well an organization can survive a disaster. This phase includes *requirements* and *strategy*. The *requirements* involve undertaking a business impact analysis and risk analysis:
   - *Requirement 1: Business Impact Analysis (BIA)* - Its purpose it to quantify the impact caused by the loss of services. If the impact can be determined in detail, it is called "hard impact" - e.g. financial losses. "Soft impact" is less easily determined. It represents, for instance, the impact on public relations, morale and health. The BIA identifies the most important services for the organization and as such provides important input for the strategy. Among other things, the analysis identifies:
     - the type of damage or loss (e.g. income, reputation)
     - how the damage could escalate
     - the required competencies, facilities and services to continue important processes

- the timeframe within which partial (the most vital processes) and full recovery must occur
- determination of recovery periods for every individual service

Generally speaking, more preventive measures need to be taken with regards to those processes and services with earlier and higher impacts. Greater emphasis should be placed on continuity and recovery measures for those where the impact is lower and takes longer to develop.

- *Requirement 2: Risk estimate* - There are various risk analysis and management methods. Risk analysis is an assessment of risks that may give rise to service disruption or security violation. Risk management identifies the response and cost-justifiable counter-measures that can be taken. A standard method like Management of Risk (M_o_R) can be used to investigate and manage the risks. This method consists of:
  - M_o_R principles
  - M_o_R approach (organization approach)
  - M_o_R processes (identification, assessment, planning, implementation)
  - M_o_R embedding and review
  - communication (up-to-date and adequate information provision)
- *Strategy 1: Risk response measures* - Measures to reduce risks must be implemented in combination with availability management since failure reduction has an impact on service availability. Measures may include: *fault tolerant systems*, good IT security controls, and *off site storage*.
- *Strategy 2: ITSCM recovery options* - The continuity strategy is a balance between the cost of risk reduction measures and recovery options to support the recovery of critical business processes within agreed timescales. A number of recovery options are possible:
  - <u>Manual workarounds</u>: temporary manual solution for a limited period of time
  - <u>Reciprocal arrangements</u>: support agreements between parties with similar infrastructures (not used often these days)
  - <u>Gradual recovery</u> (or *cold standby*): method that makes basic facilities such as accommodation and computer space available at limited costs within several days
  - <u>Intermediate recovery</u> (*warm standby*): recovery within two to three days, generally based on a prepared facility that is often shared with several other parties
  - <u>Fast recovery</u> (*hot standby*): recovery within 24 hours that focuses on the main services, involving e.g. shadow sites that can be operational very quickly and with very low data loss

  • <u>Immediate recovery</u> (also *hot standby*): option for the immediate recovery of mainly business-critical services with the aid of *mirroring* techniques, *dual sites*, and other redundancy solutions; no data loss involved

3. **Implementation** - The ITSCM plans can be created once the strategy is approved. You should remember, however, that the organization structure (leadership and decision-making processes) changes in the event of a disaster recovery process. Set this up around a senior manager generally in charge, with a coordinator below them and the recovery teams below that. Test the plans in full, e.g. using the following test types:
   - walkthrough tests
   - full tests
   - partial test (e.g. a single service or server)
   - scenario test (testing for specific responses / scenarios)

4. **Ongoing operation** - This phase includes:
   - education, awareness and training of personnel
   - review
   - testing
   - change management (ensures that all changes have been assessed for their potential impact)
   - ultimate test (invocation)

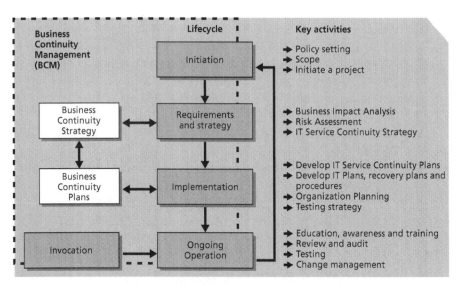

Figure 5.8 The lifecycle of IT Service Continuity Management (ITSCM)

Information management

Record all of the information that is required to maintain the ITSCM plans. Align the plan with the BCM (Business Continuity Management) information. At the very least, it should contain information about:

- the most recent version of the BCM strategy and business impact analysis
- risks within a risk register including, risk assessment and possible responses to these
- executed and planned tests
- details of the ITSCM and related plans
- existing recovery facilities, suppliers, partners and agreements
- details on backup and restore processes

Interfaces

ITSCM can be **triggered** by various events:

- new or changed business needs
- new or changed targets in the agreements e.g. SLAs, OLAs or contracts
- occurrence of a major incident that requires assessment for potential invocation of ITSCM or BCM plans
- periodical activities, such as business impact analysis or risk analysis

It has **interfaces** with, for example:

- **Incident and problem management** - Incidents and problems can easily evolve into major incidents and disasters.
- **Availability management** - Undertaking risk analysis and implementing risk response should be closely coordinated with the availability management process.
- **Service level management** - Recovery requirements are agreed and documented in SLAs.

ITSCM's **input** includes:

- business information (organization strategy, plans)
- IT information
- financial information
- BCM strategy and plans
- change information (from change management)
- CMS
- testing schedules

ITSCM **outputs** include:

- revised ITSCM policy and strategy
- business impact analysis exercises and reports

- risk analysis and management reviews and reports
- continuity plans
- test scenarios
- test reports and reviews

Metrics

ITSCM's success can be measured by the following **KPIs**:

- the outcome of regular audits of the ITSCM plans
- the extent to which service recovery targets are agreed and documented in the SLA
- the test results of the ITSCM plans
- the regular review of the ITSCM plans

Implementation

The following **challenges** apply for ITSCM:

- providing continuity plans when there is no BCM process
- if there is a BCM process, the challenge is to integrate the ITSCM plan with it and keep it that way

The **success** of ITSCM is influenced strongly by the question whether:

- services can be delivered and restored in accordance with the customer's objectives
- the entire organization is aware of the BCM and ITSCM plans

Its **risks** include:

- lack of commitment from the business and management
- lack of resources and budget
- excessive focus on technology and not on services and the customers' needs
- risk investigation and management are executed in isolation, not in collaboration with availability management and security management

5.6 Information Security Management

Introduction

The **goal** of information security management is to align IT and business security and ensure that information security is managed effectively in all services and service management activities.

Its **objectives** are:
- information is available and usable when required (availability)
- information is available exclusively to authorized persons (confidentiality)
- the information is complete, accurate and protected against unauthorized changes (integrity)
- transactions and information exchange between companies and partners can be trusted (authenticity and non-repudiation)

Scope

Information security management needs to understand the total IT and business security environment. This means, among other things:
- the current and future business security policy and plans
- security requirements
- legal requirements
- obligations and responsibilities
- business and IT risks (and their management)

This enables information security management to manage the current and future security aspects of the business cost effectively. The process should include the following elements:
- production, maintenance, distribution and enforcement of an information security policy
- understanding agreed current and future security requirements of the business
- implementing (and documenting) controls that support the information security policy and manage risks
- managing IT service providers and contracts concerning access to the system and services
- management of security breaches and incidents
- proactive improvement of the security control systems

Value for the business
Information security management ensures that the information security policy complies with the overall business security policy of the organization and the requirements of corporate governance. It raises internal awareness of the need for security within all services and assets. Executive management is responsible for organizations information and is tasked with responding to issues that affect its protection. Boards of directors are expected to make information security an integral part of corporate governance. All IT service provider organizations must therefore ensure that they have a comprehensive information security management policy in place to monitor and enforce the policies.

Basic concepts
The information security management process and framework include:
• information security policy
• Information Security Management System (ISMS)
• comprehensive security strategy (related to the business objectives and strategy)
• effective security organizational structure
• set of security controls to support the policy
• risk management
• monitoring processes
• communication strategy
• training and awareness strategy

Activities, methods and techniques

Information security management system
The Information Security Management System (ISMS) provides the basis for cost-effective development of an information security program that supports the business objectives. Use the four Ps of Personnel, Processes, Products (including technology) and Partners (including service providers) to ensure high levels of security are in place.

ISO 27001 is the formal standard against which organizations may seek certification of their ISMS. Figure 5.9 is based on various recommendations, including ISO 27001, and provides insight into the five elements and their objectives.

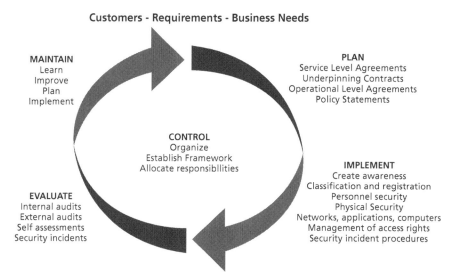

Figure 5.9 Framework for managing IT security

Security governance

IT security governance can have six outcomes:

- **strategic alignment**:
    - security requirements should be driven by enterprise requirements
    - security solutions must fit enterprise processes
- **value delivery**:
    - standard set of security practices
    - properly prioritized and distributed effort to areas with the greatest impact and business benefit
- **risk management**:
    - risk profiles
    - awareness of risk management priorities
- **performance management**:
    - defined, agreed and meaningful metrics
    - measurement process that will help that identify shortcomings
- **resource management**:
    - knowledge is recorded and available
    - security processes are documented
- **business process assurance**

The information security manager must understand that security is not merely a step in the lifecycle and that it cannot be solved by technology alone. Information security must be an integral part of all services (and systems) and is an ongoing process that needs to be continually managed. Figure 5.10 describes controls that can be used in the process.

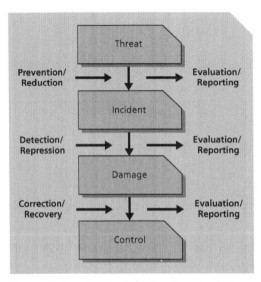

Figure 5.10 Security controls for threats and incidents

The figure shows that a risk may result in a **threat** that in turn causes an **incident**, the consequence of which is **damage**. Measures of varying nature can be taken between these phases:

- **preventive measures** - prevent effects (e.g. access management)
- **reductive measures** - limit effects (e.g. backup and testing)
- **detective measures** - detect effects (e.g. monitoring)
- **repressive measures** - suppress effects (e.g. blocking)
- **corrective measures** - repair effects (e.g. rollback)

Information management
All of the information required by information security management should be stored in an Information Security Management System (ISMS). This system includes all security controls, risks, failures, processes and reports necessary to support and maintain the information security policy and the information security management system. The information must cover all IT services and be integrated with other IT management systems, particularly the service portfolio and the CMS.

Interfaces

Security management can be **triggered** by:

- new or changed company policy
- new or changed business security policy
- new or changed corporate risk management processes
- changed or new business requirements or needs in the agreements - SLAs, OLAs or contracts

Security management has **interfaces** with, among other things:

- **Incident and problem management** - Information security management provides support in the decision-making process relating to and the correction of security incidents and problems.
- **ITSCM** - Information security management has a relationship in reviewing the impact and risks for the company, as well as the provision of recovery mechanisms. ISO 27001 requires a functioning ITSCM plan.
- **SLM** - This provides support for the establishment of security requirements and responsibilities and their inclusion in the SLR and SLA.
- **Change management** - Information security management supports change management in determining the possible impact of changes on security.

Input for the information security management process is:

- business information (strategy, plans)
- corporate governance and business security policies and guidelines
- IT information
- service information from the SLM process
- risk analysis processes and reports
- details of security events and breaches
- change information from the change management process
- CMS
- details of partner and service provider access

Output of the information security management process is:

- overall information security management policy
- ISMS
- revised security risk assessment processes and reports
- security controls, audits and reports
- security test schedules

Metrics
KPIs include:
- percentage decrease in security breaches
- percentage decrease in the impact of security breaches and incidents
- increasing awareness of security procedures in the organization

Implementation
The main **challenge** in this process is to ensure adequate support of the company, business security and senior management. If this is missing, it is impossible to establish an effective security process. If there is senior IT management support but no business support, IT security controls and risk assessment will be severely limited in what they can achieve.

If there is a business security policy established then a challenge becomes one of integration and alignment. Strict change management and configuration management are required to maintain such integration.

The **success** of information security management is influenced strongly by:
- business protected against *security violations*
- determination of a clear policy integrated with the business needs
- security procedures that are justified and supported by the senior management
- effective marketing and education in security requirements
- an improvement mechanism

Risks in information security management include:
- increased danger of information system abuse in terms of privacy and ethics
- danger of hackers
- lack of commitment from the company, senior management, lack of adequate information
- excessive focus on technical aspects and no focus on service and the customer's needs

Too often research into and management of risks is undertaking in isolation instead of in conjunction with availability management and ITSCM.

5.7   Supplier Management

Introduction

The **goal** of the supplier management process is to manage suppliers and the services they supply, to provide seamless quality of IT service to the business, ensuring value for money.

Objectives are:
- obtain value for money from suppliers and contracts
- ensure that underpinning contracts and agreements with suppliers are aligned to business needs
- manage relationships with suppliers and their performance
- negotiate and agree contracts with suppliers
- maintain a supplier policy and a supporting supplier and contract database (SCD)

Scope

The supplier management process includes the management of all suppliers and contracts needed to support the provision of IT services to the business. The greater the contribution of a supplier, the more effort the service provider must put in managing the (relationship with the) supplier, and the more they should be involved with the development and implementation of the strategy. The smaller the supplier's value contribution, the more likely it is that the relationship will be managed mainly at an operational level. The process should include the following aspects:
- implementation and enforcement of the supplier policy
- maintenance of a supplier and contract database (SCD)
- categorizing of suppliers and contracts and risk assessment
- evaluation of contracts and suppliers
- developing, negotiating and agreement of contracts
- revising, renewing and terminating contracts

Value for the business

One of the most important goals of supplier management is to get value for money from supplier and contracts and to ensure that all targets in underpinning contracts and agreements are aligned to business needs and agreed targets within the SLAs. This ensures the delivery of end-to-end seamless, quality IT services that are aligned to the business expectation. The supplier management process should align with all corporate requirements and the requirements of all other IT and service management processes particularly information security management and ITSCM.

Basic concepts

All activities in this process should be driven by a supplier strategy and the policy from Service Strategy. Create a **Supplier and Contract Database (SCD)** to achieve consistency and effectiveness in implementing policy. Ideally, this database would be an integrated element of CMS or SKMS. The database should contain all details regarding suppliers and contracts, together with details about the type of service or product, and any information and relationship to other configuration items.

The data stored here will provide important information for activities and procedures such as:

- categorizing of suppliers
- maintenance of supplier and contract database
- evaluation and set-up of new suppliers and contracts
- establishing new suppliers
- supplier and contract management and performance
- renewed and terminated contracts

Activities, methods and techniques

In case of external suppliers, it is recommended to draw up a formal contract with clearly defined, agreed upon and documented responsibilities and goals. Manage this contract during its entire lifecycle (Figure 5.11).

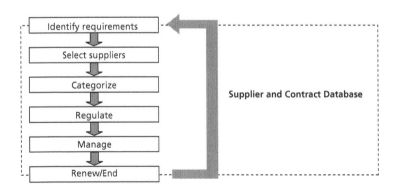

Figure 5.11 Contract lifecycle

These phases are:

1. **identify** business need and preparation of business case
   - produce a Statement of Requirement (SOR) and/or a Invitation to Tender (ITT).
   - ensure conformity to strategy and policy.
   - prepare initial business case.

2. **evaluate and procure new contracts and suppliers**
   - identify method of purchase or procurement
   - establish evaluation criteria
   - select
   - negotiate
   - agree and award contract
   - establish new suppliers and contracts
   - set up supplier service and contract within SCD
   - transition of service
   - establish contacts and relationships

3. **categorize suppliers and contracts**
   - assessment or reassessment of supplier and contract
   - ensure changes progressed through service transition
   - categorization of supplier
   - update SCD
   - maintain SCD

4. **manage the supplier and contract performance**
   - management and control of the operation and delivery of service
   - monitor and report
   - review and improve
   - management of supplier and relationship
   - review at least annually service scope against business need, targets and agreements
   - plan for possible closure

5. **end of term**
   - review
   - renegotiate and renew or terminate

Interfaces

The supplier management process can be **triggered** by:

- new or changed corporate governance guidelines
- new or changes business and IT strategies
- new or changed business requirements or changed services

Inputs to supplier management are:

- business information (strategy, plans)
- supplier and contract strategies
- business plan details
- supplier strategies
- supplier contracts
- performance information

Outputs from supplier management are:

- Supplier and Contract Database
- information about performance
- supplier improvement plans (Supplier Service Improvement Plans, SIPs)
- research reports

Relations to other processes are:

- **SLM** - assisting in determining goals, requirements and responsibilities
- **information security management** - manage suppliers and their access to services
- **Service portfolio management** - ensure that the service portfolio accurately depicts all supporting systems and details

Metrics

The performance of supplier management can be measured according to:

- the increase in the number of suppliers that meet contract agreements
- the increase in the number of contract targets aligned with the SLA and SLR

All of the information required by supplier management should be stored in the Supplier and Contract Database. This should also contain information about suppliers and contracts and the execution of supporting services. Also include the latter in the service portfolio.

Implementation

Supplier management has the following **challenges**:

- constantly changing business and IT needs

- existing imperfect contracts
- insufficient experience in the organization
- tied to long-term contracts

In order to meet these challenges, attention might be paid to the following elements:
- clearly written, well-defined service management processes on both sides
- mutually advantageous relations
- clear roles
- good communication

The **success** of supplier management will be determined in part by:
- protection against poor supplier performance
- services (and goals) adjusted to the requirements of the business
- clarity on suppliers and contracts

Supplier management has the following **risks**:
- lack of commitment from the business and senior management
- lack of information on future business goals and policy
- lack of resources or budget
- impossible contract agreements to be met

Acronyms

AMIS	Availability Management Information System
APMG	APM Group
BCM	Business Continuity Management
BCP	Business Continuity Plan
BCS	British Computer Society
BIA	Business Impact Analysis
BPO	Business Process Outsourcing
BU	Business Unit
CAB	Change Advisory Board
CCM	Component Capacity Management
CFIA	Component Failure Impact Analysis
CI	Configuration Item
CMDB	Configuration Management Database
CMIS	Capacity Management Information System
CMS	Configuration Management System
CS	Change Schedule
CSF	Critical Success Factor
CSI	Continual Service Improvement
CSP	Core Service Package
DIKW	Data Information Knowledge Wisdom
DML	Definitive Media Library
ECAB	Emergency Change Advisory Board
ELS	Early Life Support
FTA	Fault Tree Analysis

HR	Human Resources
ISMS	Information Security Management System
ITIL	Information Technology Infrastructure Library
ITSCM	IT Service Continuity Management
itSMF	IT Service Management Forum
KEDB	Known Error Database
KPI	Key Performance Indicator
KPO	Knowledge Process Outsourcing
LCS	Loyalist Certification Services
LOS	Line of Service
M_o_R	Management of Risk
MTBF	Mean Time Between Failures
MTBSI	Mean Time Between Service Incidents
MTTR	Mean Time To Repair
MTRS	Mean Time to Restore Service
OGC	Office of Government Commerce
OLA	Operational Level Agreement
PBA	Pattern of Business Activity
PDCA	Plan Do Check Act
PFS	Prerequisites for Success
PIR	Post-Implementation Review
PRINCE2	PRojects IN Controlled Environments
PSA	Projected Service Availability
PSO	Projected Service Outage
RAD	Rapid Application Development
RFC	Request for Change
SAC	Service Acceptance Criteria
SACM	Service Asset and Configuration Management
SCD	Supplier and Contract Database
SCM	Service Catalogue Management
SDP	Service Design Package
SFA	Service Failure Analysis
SIP	Service Improvement Plan
SKMS	Service Knowledge Management System
SLA	Service Level Agreement
SLM	Service Level Management
SLP	Service Level Package
SLR	Service Level Requirement
SOC	Separation of Concerns

SPM	Service Portfolio Management
SPOC	Single Point of Contact
SPOF	Single Point of Failure
TCU	Total Cost of Utilization
TSO	The Stationary Office
UC	Underpinning Contract
VBF	Vital Business Function
VCD	Variable Cost Dynamics

Glossary

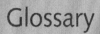

Where a term is relevant to a particular phase in the Lifecycle of an IT Service, or to one of the Core ITIL publications, this is indicated at the beginning of the definition. This glossary is based on the official ITIL V3 Glossary, version 01 of 30 May 2007.

Acceptance	Formal agreement that an IT Service, Process, Plan, or other Deliverable is complete, accurate, Reliable and meets its specified Requirements. Acceptance is usually preceded by Evaluation or Testing and is often required before proceeding to the next stage of a Project or Process. See Service Acceptance Criteria.
Access Management	(Service Operation) The Process responsible for allowing Users to make use of IT Services, data, or other Assets. Access Management helps to protect the Confidentiality, Integrity and Availability of Assets by ensuring that only authorized Users are able to access or modify the Assets. Access Management is sometimes referred to as Rights Management or Identity Management.
Account Manager	(Service Strategy) A Role that is very similar to Business Relationship Manager, but includes more commercial aspects. Most commonly used when dealing with External Customers.
Accounting	(Service Strategy) The Process responsible for identifying actual Costs of delivering IT Services, comparing these with budgeted costs, and managing variance from the Budget.
Accredited	Officially authorized to carry out a Role. For example an Accredited body may be authorized to provide training or to conduct Audits.
Active Monitoring	(Service Operation) Monitoring of a Configuration Item or an IT Service that uses automated regular checks to discover the current status. See Passive Monitoring.

Activity	A set of actions designed to achieve a particular result. Activities are usually defined as part of Processes or Plans, and are documented in Procedures.
Agreed Service Time	(Service Design) A synonym for Service Hours, commonly used in formal calculations of Availability. See Downtime.
Agreement	A Document that describes a formal understanding between two or more parties. An Agreement is not legally binding, unless it forms part of a Contract. See Service Level Agreement, Operational Level Agreement.
Alert	(Service Operation) A warning that a threshold has been reached, something has changed, or a Failure has occurred. Alerts are often created and managed by System Management tools and are managed by the Event Management Process.
Analytical Modeling	(Service Strategy) (Service Design) (Continual Service Improvement) A technique that uses mathematical Models to predict the behavior of a Configuration Item or IT Service. Analytical Models are commonly used in Capacity Management and Availability Management. See Modeling.
Application	Software that provides Functions that are required by an IT Service. Each Application may be part of more than one IT Service. An Application runs on one or more Servers or Clients. See Application Management, Application Portfolio.
Application Management	(Service Design) (Service Operation) The Function responsible for managing Applications throughout their Lifecycle.
Application Portfolio	(Service Design) A database or structured Document used to manage Applications throughout their Lifecycle. The Application Portfolio contains key Attributes of all Applications. The Application Portfolio is sometimes implemented as part of the Service Portfolio, or as part of the Configuration Management System.
Application Service Provider (ASP)	(Service Design) An External Service Provider that provides IT Services using Applications running at the Service Provider's premises. Users access the Applications by network connections to the Service Provider.
Application Sizing	(Service Design) The Activity responsible for understanding the Resource Requirements needed to support a new Application, or a major Change to an existing Application. Application Sizing helps to ensure that the IT Service can meet its agreed Service Level Targets for Capacity and Performance.
Architecture	(Service Design) The structure of a System or IT Service, including the Relationships of Components to each other and to the environment they are in. Architecture also includes the Standards and Guidelines which guide the design and evolution of the System.
Assembly	(Service Transition) A Configuration Item that is made up from a number of other CIs. For example a Server CI may contain CIs for CPUs, Disks, Memory etc.; an IT Service CI may contain many Hardware, Software and other CIs. See Component CI, Build.

Assessment	Inspection and analysis to check whether a Standard or set of Guidelines is being followed, that Records are accurate, or that Efficiency and Effectiveness targets are being met. See Audit.
Asset	(Service Strategy) Any Resource or Capability. Assets of a Service Provider include anything that could contribute to the delivery of a Service. Assets can be one of the following types: Management, Organization, Process, Knowledge, People, Information, Applications, Infrastructure, and Financial Capital.
Asset Management	(Service Transition) Asset Management is the Process responsible for tracking and reporting the value and ownership of financial Assets throughout their Lifecycle. Asset Management is part of an overall Service Asset and Configuration Management Process. See Asset Register.
Asset Register	(Service Transition) A list of Assets, which includes their ownership and value. The Asset Register is maintained by Asset Management.
Attribute	(Service Transition) A piece of information about a Configuration Item. Examples are name, location, Version number, and Cost. Attributes of CIs are recorded in the Configuration Management Database (CMDB). See Relationship.
Audit	Formal inspection and verification to check whether a Standard or set of Guidelines is being followed, that Records are accurate, or that Efficiency and Effectiveness targets are being met. An Audit may be carried out by internal or external groups. See Certification, Assessment.
Authority Matrix	Synonym for RACI.
Automatic Call Distribution (ACD)	(Service Operation) Use of Information Technology to direct an incoming telephone call to the most appropriate person in the shortest possible time. ACD is sometimes called Automated Call Distribution.
Availability	(Service Design) Ability of a Configuration Item or IT Service to perform its agreed Function when required. Availability is determined by Reliability, Maintainability, Serviceability, Performance, and Security. Availability is usually calculated as a percentage. This calculation is often based on Agreed Service Time and Downtime. It is Best Practice to calculate Availability using measurements of the Business output of the IT Service.
Availability Management	(Service Design) The Process responsible for defining, analyzing, Planning, measuring and improving all aspects of the Availability of IT Services. Availability Management is responsible for ensuring that all IT Infrastructure, Processes, Tools, Roles etc are appropriate for the agreed Service Level Targets for Availability.

Availability Management Information System (AMIS)	(Service Design) A virtual repository of all Availability Management data, usually stored in multiple physical locations. See Service Knowledge Management System.
Availability Plan	(Service Design) A Plan to ensure that existing and future Availability Requirements for IT Services can be provided Cost Effectively.
Back-out	Synonym for Remediation.
Backup	(Service Design) (Service Operation) Copying data to protect against loss of Integrity or Availability of the original.
Balanced Scorecard	(Continual Service Improvement) A management tool developed by Drs. Robert Kaplan (Harvard Business School) and David Norton. A Balanced Scorecard enables a Strategy to be broken down into Key Performance Indicators. Performance against the KPIs is used to demonstrate how well the Strategy is being achieved. A Balanced Scorecard has 4 major areas, each of which has a small number of KPIs. The same 4 areas are considered at different levels of detail throughout the Organization.
Baseline	(Continual Service Improvement) A Benchmark used as a reference point. For example:
	• An ITSM Baseline can be used as a starting point to measure the effect of a Service Improvement Plan
	• A Performance Baseline can be used to measure changes in Performance over the lifetime of an IT Service
	• A Configuration Management Baseline can be used to enable the IT Infrastructure to be restored to a known Configuration if a Change or Release fails
Benchmark	(Continual Service Improvement) The recorded state of something at a specific point in time. A Benchmark can be created for a Configuration, a Process, or any other set of data. For example, a benchmark can be used in:
	• Continual Service Improvement, to establish the current state for managing improvements.
	• Capacity Management, to document Performance characteristics during normal operations.
	• See Benchmarking, Baseline.
Benchmarking	(Continual Service Improvement) Comparing a Benchmark with a Baseline or with Best Practice. The term Benchmarking is also used to mean creating a series of Benchmarks over time, and comparing the results to measure progress or improvement.
Best Practice	Proven Activities or Processes that have been successfully used by multiple Organizations. ITIL is an example of Best Practice.
Brainstorming	(Service Design) A technique that helps a team to generate ideas. Ideas are not reviewed during the Brainstorming session, but at a later stage. Brainstorming is often used by Problem Management to identify possible causes.

British Standards Institution (BSI)	The UK National Standards body, responsible for creating and maintaining British Standards. See http://www.bsi-global.com for more information. See ISO.
Budget	A list of all the money an Organization or Business Unit plans to receive, and plans to pay out, over a specified period of time. See Budgeting, Planning.
Budgeting	The Activity of predicting and controlling the spending of money. Consists of a periodic negotiation cycle to set future Budgets (usually annual) and the day-to-day monitoring and adjusting of current Budgets.
Build	(Service Transition) The Activity of assembling a number of Configuration Items to create part of an IT Service. The term Build is also used to refer to a Release that is authorized for distribution. For example Server Build or laptop Build. See Configuration Baseline.
Build Environment	(Service Transition) A controlled Environment where Applications, IT Services and other Builds are assembled prior to being moved into a Test or Live Environment.
Business	(Service Strategy) An overall corporate entity or Organization formed of a number of Business Units. In the context of ITSM, the term Business includes public sector and not-for-profit organizations, as well as companies. An IT Service Provider provides IT Services to a Customer within a Business. The IT Service Provider may be part of the same Business as their Customer (Internal Service Provider), or part of another Business (External Service Provider).
Business Capacity Management (BCM)	(Service Design) In the context of ITSM, Business Capacity Management is the Activity responsible for understanding future Business Requirements for use in the Capacity Plan. See Service Capacity Management.
Business Case	(Service Strategy) Justification for a significant item of expenditure. Includes information about Costs, benefits, options, issues, Risks, and possible problems. See Cost Benefit Analysis.
Business Continuity Management (BCM)	(Service Design) The Business Process responsible for managing Risks that could seriously impact the Business. BCM safeguards the interests of key stakeholders, reputation, brand and value creating activities. The BCM Process involves reducing Risks to an acceptable level and planning for the recovery of Business Processes should a disruption to the Business occur. BCM sets the Objectives, Scope and Requirements for IT Service Continuity Management.
Business Continuity Plan (BCP)	(Service Design) A Plan defining the steps required to Restore Business Processes following a disruption. The Plan will also identify the triggers for Invocation, people to be involved, communications etc. IT Service Continuity Plans form a significant part of Business Continuity Plans.
Business Customer	(Service Strategy) A recipient of a product or a Service from the Business. For example if the Business is a car manufacturer then the Business Customer is someone who buys a car.

Business Impact Analysis (BIA)	(Service Strategy) BIA is the Activity in Business Continuity Management that identifies Vital Business Functions and their dependencies. These dependencies may include Suppliers, people, other Business Processes, IT Services etc. BIA defines the recovery requirements for IT Services. These requirements include Recovery Time Objectives, Recovery Point Objectives and minimum Service Level Targets for each IT Service.
Business Objective	(Service Strategy) The Objective of a Business Process, or of the Business as a whole. Business Objectives support the Business Vision, provide guidance for the IT Strategy, and are often supported by IT Services.
Business Operations	(Service Strategy) The day-to-day execution, monitoring and management of Business Processes.
Business Perspective	(Continual Service Improvement) An understanding of the Service Provider and IT Services from the point of view of the Business, and an understanding of the Business from the point of view of the Service Provider.
Business Process	A Process that is owned and carried out by the Business. A Business Process contributes to the delivery of a product or Service to a Business Customer. For example, a retailer may have a purchasing Process which helps to deliver Services to their Business Customers. Many Business Processes rely on IT Services.
Business Relationship Management	(Service Strategy) The Process or Function responsible for maintaining a Relationship with the Business. BRM usually includes: • Managing personal Relationships with Business managers • Providing input to Service Portfolio Management • Ensuring that the IT Service Provider is satisfying the Business needs of the Customers This Process has strong links with Service Level Management.
Business Relationship Manager (BRM)	(Service Strategy) A Role responsible for maintaining the Relationship with one or more Customers. This Role is often combined with the Service Level Manager Role. See Account Manager.
Business Service	An IT Service that directly supports a Business Process, as opposed to an Infrastructure Service which is used internally by the IT Service Provider and is not usually visible to the Business. The term Business Service is also used to mean a Service that is delivered to Business Customers by Business Units. For example delivery of financial services to Customers of a bank, or goods to the Customers of a retail store. Successful delivery of Business Services often depends on one or more IT Services.
Business Service Management (BSM)	(Service Strategy) (Service Design) An approach to the management of IT Services that considers the Business Processes supported and the Business value provided. This term also means the management of Business Services delivered to Business Customers.

Business Unit

(Service Strategy) A segment of the Business which has its own Plans, Metrics, income and Costs. Each Business Unit owns Assets and uses these to create value for Customers in the form of goods and Services.

Call

(Service Operation) A telephone call to the Service Desk from a User. A Call could result in an Incident or a Service Request being logged.

Call Centre

(Service Operation) An Organization or Business Unit which handles large numbers of incoming and outgoing telephone calls.
See Service Desk.

Call Type

(Service Operation) A Category that is used to distinguish incoming requests to a Service Desk. Common Call Types are Incident, Service Request and Complaint.

Capability

(Service Strategy) The ability of an Organization, person, Process, Application, Configuration Item or IT Service to carry out an Activity. Capabilities are intangible Assets of an Organization.
See Resource.

Capability Maturity Model (CMM)

(Continual Service Improvement) The Capability Maturity Model for Software (also known as the CMM and SW-CMM) is a model used to identify Best Practices to help increase Process Maturity. CMM was developed at the Software Engineering Institute (SEI) of Carnegie Mellon University. In 2000, the SW-CMM was upgraded to CMMI® (Capability Maturity Model Integration). The SEI no longer maintains the SW-CMM model, its associated appraisal methods, or training materials.

Capability Maturity Model Integration (CMMI)

(Continual Service Improvement) Capability Maturity Model® Integration (CMMI) is a process improvement approach developed by the Software Engineering Institute (SEI) of Carnegie Melon University. CMMI provides organizations with the essential elements of effective processes. It can be used to guide process improvement across a project, a division, or an entire organization. CMMI helps integrate traditionally separate organizational functions, set process improvement goals and priorities, provide guidance for quality processes, and provide a point of reference for appraising current processes.
See http://www.sei.cmu.edu/cmmi/ for more information.
See CMM, Continuous Improvement, Maturity.

Capacity

(Service Design) The maximum Throughput that a Configuration Item or IT Service can deliver whilst meeting agreed Service Level Targets. For some types of CI, Capacity may be the size or volume, for example a disk drive.

Capacity Management

(Service Design) The Process responsible for ensuring that the Capacity of IT Services and the IT Infrastructure is able to deliver agreed Service Level Targets in a Cost Effective and timely manner. Capacity Management considers all Resources required to deliver the IT Service, and plans for short, medium and long term Business Requirements.

Capacity Management Information System (CMIS)
: (Service Design) A virtual repository of all Capacity Management data, usually stored in multiple physical locations.
See Service Knowledge Management System.

Capacity Plan
: (Service Design) A Capacity Plan is used to manage the Resources required to deliver IT Services. The Plan contains scenarios for different predictions of Business demand, and costed options to deliver the agreed Service Level Targets.

Capacity Planning
: (Service Design) The Activity within Capacity Management responsible for creating a Capacity Plan.

Capital Expenditure (CAPEX)
: (Service Strategy) The Cost of purchasing something that will become a financial Asset, for example computer equipment and buildings. The value of the Asset is Depreciated over multiple accounting periods.

Capital Item
: (Service Strategy) An Asset that is of interest to Financial Management because it is above an agreed financial value.

Capitalization
: (Service Strategy) Identifying major Cost as capital, even though no Asset is purchased. This is done to spread the impact of the Cost over multiple accounting periods. The most common example of this is software development, or purchase of a software license.

Category
: A named group of things that have something in common. Categories are used to group similar things together. For example Cost Types are used to group similar types of Cost. Incident Categories are used to group similar types of Incident, CI Types are used to group similar types of Configuration Item.

Certification
: Issuing a certificate to confirm Compliance to a Standard. Certification includes a formal Audit by an independent and Accredited body. The term Certification is also used to mean awarding a certificate to verify that a person has achieved a qualification.

Change
: (Service Transition) The addition, modification or removal of anything that could have an effect on IT Services. The Scope should include all IT Services, Configuration Items, Processes, Documentation etc.

Change Advisory Board (CAB)
: (Service Transition) A group of people that advises the Change Manager in the Assessment, prioritization and scheduling of Changes. This board is usually made up of representatives from all areas within the IT Service Provider, the Business, and Third Parties such as Suppliers.

Change Case
: (Service Operation) A technique used to predict the impact of proposed Changes. Change Cases use specific scenarios to clarify the scope of proposed Changes and to help with Cost Benefit Analysis.
See Use Case.

Change History	(Service Transition) Information about all changes made to a Configuration Item during its life. Change History consists of all those Change Records that apply to the CI.
Change Management	(Service Transition) The Process responsible for controlling the Lifecycle of all Changes. The primary objective of Change Management is to enable beneficial Changes to be made, with minimum disruption to IT Services.
Change Model	(Service Transition) A repeatable way of dealing with a particular Category of Change. A Change Model defines specific pre-defined steps that will be followed for a Change of this Category. Change Models may be very simple, with no requirement for approval (e.g. Password Reset) or may be very complex with many steps that require approval (e.g. major software Release). See Standard Change, Change Advisory Board.
Change Record	(Service Transition) A Record containing the details of a Change. Each Change Record documents the Lifecycle of a single Change. A Change Record is created for every Request for Change that is received, even those that are subsequently rejected. Change Records should reference the Configuration Items that are affected by the Change. Change Records are stored in the Configuration Management System.
Change Request	Synonym for Request for Change.
Change Schedule	(Service Transition) A Document that lists all approved Changes and their planned implementation dates. A Change Schedule is sometimes called a Forward Schedule of Change, even though it also contains information about Changes that have already been implemented.
Change Window	(Service Transition) A regular, agreed time when Changes or Releases may be implemented with minimal impact on Services. Change Windows are usually documented in SLAs.
Charging	(Service Strategy) Requiring payment for IT Services. Charging for IT Services is optional, and many Organizations choose to treat their IT Service Provider as a Cost Centre.
Chronological Analysis	(Service Operation) A technique used to help identify possible causes of Problems. All available data about the Problem is collected and sorted by date and time to provide a detailed timeline. This can make it possible to identify which Events may have been triggered by others.
CI Type	(Service Transition) A Category that is used to Classify CIs. The CI Type identifies the required Attributes and Relationships for a Configuration Record. Common CI Types include: hardware, Document, User etc.
Classification	The act of assigning a Category to something. Classification is used to ensure consistent management and reporting. CIs, Incidents, Problems, Changes etc. are usually classified.

Client

A generic term that means a Customer, the Business or a Business Customer. For example Client Manager may be used as a synonym for Account Manager.
The term client is also used to mean:
- A computer that is used directly by a User, for example a PC, Handheld Computer, or Workstation.
- The part of a Client-Server Application that the User directly interfaces with. For example an email Client.

Closed

(Service Operation) The final Status in the Lifecycle of an Incident, Problem, Change etc. When the Status is Closed, no further action is taken.

Closure

(Service Operation) The act of changing the Status of an Incident, Problem, Change etc. to Closed.

COBIT

(Continual Service Improvement) Control Objectives for Information and related Technology (COBIT) provides guidance and Best Practice for the management of IT Processes. COBIT is published by the IT Governance Institute.
See http://www.isaca.org/ for more information.

Code of Practice

A Guideline published by a public body or a Standards Organization, such as ISO or BSI. Many Standards consist of a Code of Practice and a Specification. The Code of Practice describes recommended Best Practice.

Cold Standby

Synonym for Gradual Recovery.

Commercial off the Shelf (COTS)

(Service Design) Application software or Middleware that can be purchased from a Third Party.

Compliance

Ensuring that a Standard or set of Guidelines is followed, or that proper, consistent accounting or other practices are being employed.

Component

A general term that is used to mean one part of something more complex. For example, a computer System may be a component of an IT Service, an Application may be a Component of a Release Unit. Components that need to be managed should be Configuration Items.

Component Capacity Management (CCM)

(Service Design) (Continual Service Improvement) The Process responsible for understanding the Capacity, Utilization, and Performance of Configuration Items. Data is collected, recorded and analyzed for use in the Capacity Plan.
See Service Capacity Management.

Component CI

(Service Transition) A Configuration Item that is part of an Assembly. For example, a CPU or Memory CI may be part of a Server CI.

Component Failure Impact Analysis (CFIA)

(Service Design) A technique that helps to identify the impact of CI failure on IT Services. A matrix is created with IT Services on one edge and CIs on the other. This enables the identification of critical CIs (that could cause the failure of multiple IT Services) and of fragile IT Services (that have multiple Single Points of Failure).

Computer Telephony Integration (CTI)	(Service Operation) CTI is a general term covering any kind of integration between computers and telephone Systems. It is most commonly used to refer to Systems where an Application displays detailed screens relating to incoming or outgoing telephone calls. See Automatic Call Distribution, Interactive Voice Response.
Concurrency	A measure of the number of Users engaged in the same Operation at the same time.
Confidentiality	(Service Design) A security principle that requires that data should only be accessed by authorized people.
Configuration	(Service Transition) A generic term, used to describe a group of Configuration Items that work together to deliver an IT Service, or a recognizable part of an IT Service. Configuration is also used to describe the parameter settings for one or more CIs.
Configuration Baseline	(Service Transition) A Baseline of a Configuration that has been formally agreed and is managed through the Change Management process. A Configuration Baseline is used as a basis for future Builds, Releases and Changes.
Configuration Control	(Service Transition) The Activity responsible for ensuring that adding, modifying or removing a CI is properly managed, for example by submitting a Request for Change or Service Request.
Configuration Identification	(Service Transition) The Activity responsible for collecting information about Configuration Items and their Relationships, and loading this information into the CMDB. Configuration Identification is also responsible for labeling the CIs themselves, so that the corresponding Configuration Records can be found.
Configuration Item (CI)	(Service Transition) Any Component that needs to be managed in order to deliver an IT Service. Information about each CI is recorded in a Configuration Record within the Configuration Management System and is maintained throughout its Lifecycle by Configuration Management. CIs are under the control of Change Management. CIs typically include IT Services, hardware, software, buildings, people, and formal documentation such as Process documentation and SLAs.
Configuration Management	(Service Transition) The Process responsible for maintaining information about Configuration Items required to deliver an IT Service, including their Relationships. This information is managed throughout the Lifecycle of the CI. Configuration Management is part of an overall Service Asset and Configuration Management Process.
Configuration Management Database (CMDB)	(Service Transition) A database used to store Configuration Records throughout their Lifecycle. The Configuration Management System maintains one or more CMDBs, and each CMDB stores Attributes of CIs, and Relationships with other CIs.

Configuration Management System (CMS)	(Service Transition) A set of tools and databases that are used to manage an IT Service Provider's Configuration data. The CMS also includes information about Incidents, Problems, Known Errors, Changes and Releases; and may contain data about employees, Suppliers, locations, Business Units, Customers and Users. The CMS includes tools for collecting, storing, managing, updating, and presenting data about all Configuration Items and their Relationships. The CMS is maintained by Configuration Management and is used by all IT Service Management Processes. See Configuration Management Database, Service Knowledge Management System.
Configuration Record	(Service Transition) A Record containing the details of a Configuration Item. Each Configuration Record documents the Lifecycle of a single CI. Configuration Records are stored in a Configuration Management Database.
Configuration Structure	(Service Transition) The hierarchy and other Relationships between all the Configuration Items that comprise a Configuration.
Continual Service Improvement (CSI)	(Continual Service Improvement) A stage in the Lifecycle of an IT Service and the title of one of the Core ITIL publications. Continual Service Improvement is responsible for managing improvements to IT Service Management Processes and IT Services. The Performance of the IT Service Provider is continually measured and improvements are made to Processes, IT Services and IT Infrastructure in order to increase Efficiency, Effectiveness, and Cost Effectiveness. See Plan-Do-Check-Act.
Continuous Availability	(Service Design) An approach or design to achieve 100% Availability. A Continuously Available IT Service has no planned or unplanned Downtime.
Continuous Operation	(Service Design) An approach or design to eliminate planned Downtime of an IT Service. Note that individual Configuration Items may be down even though the IT Service is Available.
Contract	A legally binding Agreement between two or more parties.
Contract Portfolio	(Service Strategy) A database or structured Document used to manage Service Contracts or Agreements between an IT Service Provider and their Customers. Each IT Service delivered to a Customer should have a Contract or other Agreement which is listed in the Contract Portfolio. See Service Portfolio, Service Catalogue.
Control	A means of managing a Risk, ensuring that a Business Objective is achieved, or ensuring that a Process is followed. Example Controls include Policies, Procedures, Roles, RAID, door-locks etc. A control is sometimes called a Countermeasure or safeguard. Control also means to manage the utilization or behavior of a Configuration Item, System or IT Service.

Control Objectives for Information and related Technology (COBIT)	See COBIT.
Control perspective	(Service Strategy) An approach to the management of IT Services, Processes, Functions, Assets etc. There can be several different Control Perspectives on the same IT Service, Process etc., allowing different individuals or teams to focus on what is important and relevant to their specific Role. Example Control Perspectives include Reactive and Proactive management within IT Operations, or a Lifecycle view for an Application Project team.
Control Processes	The ISO/IEC 20000 Process group that includes Change Management and Configuration Management.
Core Service	(Service Strategy) An IT Service that delivers basic Outcomes desired by one or more Customers. See Supporting Service, Core Service Package.
Core Service Package (CSP)	(Service Strategy) A detailed description of a Core Service that may be shared by two or more Service Level Packages. See Service Package.
Cost	The amount of money spent on a specific Activity, IT Service, or Business Unit. Costs consist of real cost (money), notional cost such as people's time, and Depreciation.
Cost Benefit Analysis	An Activity that analyses and compares the Costs and the benefits involved in one or more alternative courses of action. See Business Case, Net Present Value, Internal Rate of Return, Return on Investment, Value on Investment.
Cost Centre	(Service Strategy) A Business Unit or Project to which Costs are assigned. A Cost Centre does not charge for Services provided. An IT Service Provider can be run as a Cost Centre or a Profit Centre.
Cost Effectiveness	A measure of the balance between the Effectiveness and Cost of a Service, Process or activity, A Cost Effective Process is one which achieves its Objectives at minimum Cost. See KPI, Return on Investment, Value for Money.
Cost Element	(Service Strategy) The middle level of category to which Costs are assigned in Budgeting and Accounting. The highest level category is Cost Type. For example a Cost Type of "people" could have cost elements of payroll, staff benefits, expenses, training, overtime etc. Cost Elements can be further broken down to give Cost Units. For example the Cost Element "expenses" could include Cost Units of Hotels, Transport, Meals etc.
Cost Management	(Service Strategy) A general term that is used to refer to Budgeting and Accounting, sometimes used as a synonym for Financial Management

Cost Type	(Service Strategy) The highest level of category to which Costs are assigned in Budgeting and Accounting. For example hardware, software, people, accommodation, external and Transfer. See Cost Element, Cost Type.
Cost Unit	(Service Strategy) The lowest level of category to which Costs are assigned, Cost Units are usually things that can be easily counted (e.g. staff numbers, software licenses) or things easily measured (e.g. CPU usage, Electricity consumed). Cost Units are included within Cost Elements. For example a Cost Element of "expenses" could include Cost Units of Hotels, Transport, Meals etc. See Cost Type.
Countermeasure	Can be used to refer to any type of Control. The term Countermeasure is most often used when referring to measures that increase Resilience, Fault Tolerance or Reliability of an IT Service.
Course Corrections	Changes made to a Plan or Activity that has already started, to ensure that it will meet its Objectives. Course corrections are made as a result of Monitoring progress.
CRAMM	A methodology and tool for analyzing and managing Risks. CRAMM was developed by the UK Government, but is now privately owned. Further information is available from http://www.cramm.com/
Crisis Management	The Process responsible for managing the wider implications of Business Continuity. A Crisis Management team is responsible for Strategic issues such as managing media relations and shareholder confidence, and decides when to invoke Business Continuity Plans.
Critical Success Factor (CSF)	Something that must happen if a Process, Project, Plan, or IT Service is to succeed. KPIs are used to measure the achievement of each CSF. For example a CSF of "protect IT Services when making Changes" could be measured by KPIs such as "percentage reduction of unsuccessful Changes", "percentage reduction in Changes causing Incidents" etc.
Culture	A set of values that is shared by a group of people, including expectations about how people should behave, ideas, beliefs, and practices. See Vision.
Customer	Someone who buys goods or Services. The Customer of an IT Service Provider is the person or group who defines and agrees the Service Level Targets. The term Customers is also sometimes informally used to mean Users, for example "this is a Customer focused Organization".
Customer Portfolio	(Service Strategy) A database or structured Document used to record all Customers of the IT Service Provider. The Customer Portfolio is the Business Relationship Manager's view of the Customers who receive Services from the IT Service Provider. See Contract Portfolio, Service Portfolio.

Dashboard	(Service Operation) A graphical representation of overall IT Service Performance and Availability. Dashboard images may be updated in real-time, and can also be included in management reports and web pages. Dashboards can be used to support Service Level Management, Event Management or Incident Diagnosis.
Data-to-Information-to-Knowledge-to-Wisdom (DIKW)	A way of understanding the relationships between data, information, knowledge, and wisdom. DIKW shows how each of these builds on the others.
Definitive Media Library (DML)	(Service Transition) One or more locations in which the definitive and approved versions of all software Configuration Items are securely stored. The DML may also contain associated CIs such as licenses and documentation. The DML is a single logical storage area even if there are multiple locations. All software in the DML is under the control of Change and Release Management and is recorded in the Configuration Management System. Only software from the DML is acceptable for use in a Release.
Deliverable	Something that must be provided to meet a commitment in a Service Level Agreement or a Contract. Deliverable is also used in a more informal way to mean a planned output of any Process.
Demand Management	Activities that understand and influence Customer demand for Services and the provision of Capacity to meet these demands. At a Strategic level Demand Management can involve analysis of Patterns of Business Activity and User Profiles. At a Tactical level it can involve use of Differential Charging to encourage Customers to use IT Services at less busy times. See Capacity Management.
Deming Cycle	Synonym for Plan Do Check Act.
Dependency	The direct or indirect reliance of one Process or Activity upon another.
Deployment	(Service Transition) The Activity responsible for movement of new or changed hardware, software, documentation, Process, etc to the Live Environment. Deployment is part of the Release and Deployment Management Process. See Rollout.
Depreciation	(Service Strategy) A measure of the reduction in value of an Asset over its life. This is based on wearing out, consumption or other reduction in the useful economic value.
Design	(Service Design) An Activity or Process that identifies Requirements and then defines a solution that is able to meet these Requirements. See Service Design.
Detection	(Service Operation) A stage in the Incident Lifecycle. Detection results in the Incident becoming known to the Service Provider. Detection can be automatic, or can be the result of a User logging an Incident.

Development	(Service Design) The Process responsible for creating or modifying an IT Service or Application. Also used to mean the Role or group that carries out Development work.
Development Environment	(Service Design) An Environment used to create or modify IT Services or Applications. Development Environments are not typically subjected to the same degree of control as Test Environments or Live Environments. See Development.
Diagnosis	(Service Operation) A stage in the Incident and Problem Lifecycles. The purpose of Diagnosis is to identify a Workaround for an Incident or the Root Cause of a Problem.
Diagnostic Script	(Service Operation) A structured set of questions used by Service Desk staff to ensure they ask the correct questions, and to help them Classify, Resolve and assign Incidents. Diagnostic Scripts may also be made available to Users to help them diagnose and resolve their own Incidents.
Differential Charging	A technique used to support Demand Management by charging different amounts for the same IT Service Function at different times.
Direct Cost	(Service Strategy) A cost of providing an IT Service which can be allocated in full to a specific Customer, Cost Centre, Project etc. For example cost of providing non-shared servers or software licenses. See Indirect Cost.
Directory Service	(Service Operation) An Application that manages information about IT Infrastructure available on a network, and corresponding User access Rights.
Do Nothing	(Service Design) A Recovery Option. The Service Provider formally agrees with the Customer that Recovery of this IT Service will not be performed.
Document	Information in readable form. A Document may be paper or electronic. For example a Policy statement, Service Level Agreement, Incident Record, diagram of computer room layout. See Record.
Downtime	(Service Design) (Service Operation) The time when a Configuration Item or IT Service is not Available during its Agreed Service Time. The Availability of an IT Service is often calculated from Agreed Service Time and Downtime.
Driver	Something that influences Strategy, Objectives or Requirements. For example new legislation or the actions of competitors.
Early Life Support	(Service Transition) Support provided for a new or Changed IT Service for a period of time after it is Released. During Early Life Support the IT Service Provider may review the KPIs, Service Levels and Monitoring Thresholds, and provide additional Resources for Incident and Problem Management.

Economies of scale	(Service Strategy) The reduction in average Cost that is possible from increasing the usage of an IT Service or Asset. See Economies of Scope.
Economies of scope	(Service Strategy) The reduction in Cost that is allocated to an IT Service by using an existing Asset for an additional purpose. For example delivering a new IT Service from existing IT Infrastructure. See Economies of Scale.
Effectiveness	(Continual Service Improvement) A measure of whether the Objectives of a Process, Service or Activity have been achieved. An Effective Process or Activity is one that achieves its agreed Objectives. See KPI.
Efficiency	(Continual Service Improvement) A measure of whether the right amount of resources have been used to deliver a Process, Service or Activity. An Efficient Process achieves its Objectives with the minimum amount of time, money, people or other resources. See KPI.
Emergency Change	(Service Transition) A Change that must be introduced as soon as possible. For example to resolve a Major Incident or implement a Security patch. The Change Management Process will normally have a specific Procedure for handling Emergency Changes. See Emergency Change Advisory Board (ECAB).
Emergency Change Advisory Board (ECAB)	(Service Transition) A sub-set of the Change Advisory Board who make decisions about high impact Emergency Changes. Membership of the ECAB may be decided at the time a meeting is called, and depends on the nature of the Emergency Change.
Environment	(Service Transition) A subset of the IT Infrastructure that is used for a particular purpose. For Example: Live Environment, Test Environment, Build Environment. It is possible for multiple Environments to share a Configuration Item, for example Test and Live Environments may use different partitions on a single mainframe computer. Also used in the term Physical Environment to mean the accommodation, air conditioning, power system etc. Environment is also used as a generic term to mean the external conditions that influence or affect something.
Error	(Service Operation) A design flaw or malfunction that causes a Failure of one or more Configuration Items or IT Services. A mistake made by a person or a faulty Process that impacts a CI or IT Service is also an Error.
Escalation	(Service Operation) An Activity that obtains additional Resources when these are needed to meet Service Level Targets or Customer expectations. Escalation may be needed within any IT Service Management Process, but is most commonly associated with Incident Management, Problem Management and the management of Customer complaints. There are two types of Escalation, Functional Escalation and Hierarchic Escalation.

eSourcing Capability Model for Client Organizations (eSCM-CL)	(Service Strategy) A framework to help Organizations guide their analysis and decisions on Service Sourcing Models and Strategies. eSCM-CL was developed by Carnegie Mellon University. See eSCM-SP.
eSourcing Capability Model for Service Providers (eSCM-SP)	(Service Strategy) A framework to help IT Service Providers develop their IT Service Management Capabilities from a Service Sourcing perspective. eSCM-SP was developed by Carnegie Mellon University. See eSCM-CL.
Estimation	The use of experience to provide an approximate value for a Metric or Cost. Estimation is also used in Capacity and Availability Management as the cheapest and least accurate Modeling method.
Evaluation	(Service Transition) The Process responsible for assessing a new or Changed IT Service to ensure that Risks have been managed and to help determine whether to proceed with the Change. Evaluation is also used to mean comparing an actual Outcome with the intended Outcome, or comparing one alternative with another.
Event	(Service Operation) A change of state which has significance for the management of a Configuration Item or IT Service. The term Event is also used to mean an Alert or notification created by any IT Service, Configuration Item or Monitoring tool. Events typically require IT Operations personnel to take actions, and often lead to Incidents being logged.
Event Management	(Service Operation) The Process responsible for managing Events throughout their Lifecycle. Event Management is one of the main Activities of IT Operations.
Exception Report	A Document containing details of one or more KPIs or other important targets that have exceeded defined Thresholds. Examples include SLA targets being missed or about to be missed, and a Performance Metric indicating a potential Capacity problem.
Expanded Incident Lifecycle	(Availability Management) Detailed stages in the Lifecycle of an Incident. The stages are Detection, Diagnosis, Repair, Recovery, Restoration. The Expanded Incident Lifecycle is used to help understand all contributions to the Impact of Incidents and to Plan how these could be controlled or reduced.
External Customer	A Customer who works for a different Business to the IT Service Provider. See External Service Provider, Internal Customer.
External Metric	A Metric that is used to measure the delivery of IT Service to a Customer. External Metrics are usually defined in SLAs and reported to Customers. See Internal Metric.
External Service Provider	(Service Strategy) An IT Service Provider which is part of a different Organization to their Customer. An IT Service Provider may have both Internal Customers and External Customers. See Type III Service Provider.

External Sourcing	Synonym for Outsourcing.
Facilities Management	(Service Operation) The Function responsible for managing the physical Environment where the IT Infrastructure is located. Facilities Management includes all aspects of managing the physical Environment, for example power and cooling, building Access Management, and environmental Monitoring.
Failure	(Service Operation) Loss of ability to Operate to Specification, or to deliver the required output. The term Failure may be used when referring to IT Services, Processes, Activities, Configuration Items etc. A Failure often causes an Incident.
Failure Modes and Effects Analysis (FMEA)	An approach to assessing the potential Impact of Failures. FMEA involves analyzing what would happen after Failure of each Configuration Item, all the way up to the effect on the Business. FMEA is often used in Information Security Management and in IT Service Continuity Planning.
Fast Recovery	(Service Design) A Recovery Option which is also known as Hot Standby. Provision is made to Recover the IT Service in a short period of time, typically less than 24 hours. Fast Recovery typically uses a dedicated Fixed Facility with computer Systems, and software configured ready to run the IT Services. Immediate Recovery may take up to 24 hours if there is a need to Restore data from Backups.
Fault	Synonym for Error.
Fault Tolerance	(Service Design) The ability of an IT Service or Configuration Item to continue to Operate correctly after Failure of a Component part. See Resilience, Countermeasure.
Fault Tree Analysis (FTA)	(Service Design) (Continual Service Improvement) A technique that can be used to determine the chain of Events that leads to a Problem. Fault Tree Analysis represents a chain of Events using Boolean notation in a diagram.
Financial Management	(Service Strategy) The Function and Processes responsible for managing an IT Service Provider's Budgeting, Accounting and Charging Requirements.
First-line Support	(Service Operation) The first level in a hierarchy of Support Groups involved in the resolution of Incidents. Each level contains more specialist skills, or has more time or other Resources. See Escalation.
Fishbone Diagram	Synonym for Ishikawa Diagram.
Fit for Purpose	An informal term used to describe a Process, Configuration Item, IT Service etc. that is capable of meeting its Objectives or Service Levels. Being Fit for Purpose requires suitable Design, implementation, Control and maintenance.
Fixed Cost	(Service Strategy) A Cost that does not vary with IT Service usage. For example the cost of Server hardware. See Variable Cost.

Fixed Facility   (Service Design) A permanent building, available for use when needed by an IT
                          Service Continuity Plan.
                          See Recovery Option, Portable Facility.

Follow the Sun   (Service Operation) A methodology for using Service Desks and Support Groups
                          around the world to provide seamless 24 * 7 Service. Calls, Incidents, Problems and
                          Service Requests are passed between groups in different time zones.

Fulfilment   Performing Activities to meet a need or Requirement. For example by providing a
                          new IT Service, or meeting a Service Request.

Function   A team or group of people and the tools they use to carry out one or more
                          Processes or Activities. For example the Service Desk.
                          The term Function also has two other meanings
                          •   An intended purpose of a Configuration Item, Person, Team, Process, or IT
                               Service. For example one Function of an Email Service may be to store and
                               forward outgoing mails, one Function of a Business Process may be to dispatch
                               goods to Customers.
                          •   To perform the intended purpose correctly, "The computer is Functioning"

Functional Escalation   (Service Operation) Transferring an Incident, Problem or Change to a technical
                          team with a higher level of expertise to assist in an Escalation.

Gap Analysis   (Continual Service Improvement) An Activity which compares two sets of data
                          and identifies the differences. Gap Analysis is commonly used to compare a set of
                          Requirements with actual delivery.
                          See Benchmarking.

Governance   Ensuring that Policies and Strategy are actually implemented, and that required
                          Processes are correctly followed. Governance includes defining Roles and
                          responsibilities, measuring and reporting, and taking actions to resolve any issues
                          identified.

Gradual Recovery   (Service Design) A Recovery Option which is also known as Cold Standby.
                          Provision is made to Recover the IT Service in a period of time greater than
                          72 hours. Gradual Recovery typically uses a Portable or Fixed Facility that has
                          environmental support and network cabling, but no computer Systems. The
                          hardware and software are installed as part of the IT Service Continuity Plan.

Guideline   A Document describing Best Practice, that recommends what should be done.
                          Compliance to a guideline is not normally enforced.
                          See Standard.

Help Desk   (Service Operation) A point of contact for Users to log Incidents. A Help Desk
                          is usually more technically focused than a Service Desk and does not provide a
                          Single Point of Contact for all interaction. The term Help Desk is often used as a
                          synonym for Service Desk.

Hierarchic Escalation   (Service Operation) Informing or involving more senior levels of management to
                          assist in an Escalation.

High Availability	(Service Design) An approach or Design that minimizes or hides the effects of Configuration Item Failure on the Users of an IT Service. High Availability solutions are Designed to achieve an agreed level of Availability and make use of techniques such as Fault Tolerance, Resilience and fast Recovery to reduce the number of Incidents, and the Impact of Incidents.
Hot Standby	Synonym for Fast Recovery or Immediate Recovery.
Identity	(Service Operation) A unique name that is used to identify a User, person or Role. The Identity is used to grant Rights to that User, person, or Role. Example identities might be the username SmithJ or the Role "Change manager".
Immediate Recovery	(Service Design) A Recovery Option which is also known as Hot Standby. Provision is made to Recover the IT Service with no loss of Service. Immediate Recovery typically uses mirroring, load balancing and split site technologies.
Impact	(Service Operation) (Service Transition) A measure of the effect of an Incident, Problem or Change on Business Processes. Impact is often based on how Service Levels will be affected. Impact and Urgency are used to assign Priority.
Incident	(Service Operation) An unplanned interruption to an IT Service or a reduction in the Quality of an IT Service. Failure of a Configuration Item that has not yet impacted Service is also an Incident. For example Failure of one disk from a mirror set.
Incident Management	(Service Operation) The Process responsible for managing the Lifecycle of all Incidents. The primary Objective of Incident Management is to return the IT Service to Users as quickly as possible.
Incident Record	(Service Operation) A Record containing the details of an Incident. Each Incident record documents the Lifecycle of a single Incident.
Indirect Cost	(Service Strategy) A Cost of providing an IT Service which cannot be allocated in full to a specific Customer. For example Cost of providing shared Servers or software licenses. Also known as Overhead. See Direct Cost.
Information Security Management (ISM)	(Service Design) The Process that ensures the Confidentiality, Integrity and Availability of an Organization's Assets, information, data and IT Services. Information Security Management usually forms part of an Organizational approach to Security Management which has a wider scope than the IT Service Provider, and includes handling of paper, building access, phone calls etc., for the entire Organization.
Information Security Management System (ISMS)	(Service Design) The framework of Policy, Processes, Standards, Guidelines and tools that ensures an Organization can achieve its Information Security Management Objectives.
Information Security Policy	(Service Design) The Policy that governs the Organization's approach to Information Security Management.

Information Technology (IT)	The use of technology for the storage, communication or processing of information. The technology typically includes computers, telecommunications, Applications and other software. The information may include Business data, voice, images, video, etc. Information Technology is often used to support Business Processes through IT Services.
Infrastructure Service	An IT Service that is not directly used by the Business, but is required by the IT Service Provider so they can provide other IT Services. For example Directory Services, naming services, or communication services.
Insourcing	Synonym for Internal Sourcing.
Integrity	(Service Design) A security principle that ensures data and Configuration Items are only modified by authorized personnel and Activities. Integrity considers all possible causes of modification, including software and hardware Failure, environmental Events, and human intervention.
Interactive Voice Response (IVR)	(Service Operation) A form of Automatic Call Distribution that accepts User input, such as key presses and spoken commands, to identify the correct destination for incoming Calls.
Intermediate Recovery	(Service Design) A Recovery Option which is also known as Warm Standby. Provision is made to Recover the IT Service in a period of time between 24 and 72 hours. Intermediate Recovery typically uses a shared Portable or Fixed Facility that has computer Systems and network Components. The hardware and software will need to be configured, and data will need to be restored, as part of the IT Service Continuity Plan.
Internal Customer	A Customer who works for the same Business as the IT Service Provider. See Internal Service Provider, External Customer.
Internal Metric	A Metric that is used within the IT Service Provider to Monitor the Efficiency, Effectiveness or Cost Effectiveness of the IT Service Provider's internal Processes. Internal Metrics are not normally reported to the Customer of the IT Service. See External Metric.
Internal Rate of Return (IRR)	(Service Strategy) A technique used to help make decisions about Capital Expenditure. IRR calculates a figure that allows two or more alternative investments to be compared. A larger IRR indicates a better investment. See Net Present Value, Return on Investment.
Internal Service Provider	(Service Strategy) An IT Service Provider which is part of the same Organization as their Customer. An IT Service Provider may have both Internal Customers and External Customers. See Type I Service Provider, Type II Service Provider, Insource.
Internal Sourcing	(Service Strategy) Using an Internal Service Provider to manage IT Services. See Service Sourcing, Type I Service Provider, Type II Service Provider.

International Organization for Standardization (ISO)	The International Organization for Standardization (ISO) is the world's largest developer of Standards. ISO is a non-governmental organization which is a network of the national standards institutes of 156 countries. Further information about ISO is available from http://www.iso.org/
International Standards Organization	See International Organization for Standardization (ISO)
Internet Service Provider (ISP)	An External Service Provider that provides access to the Internet. Most ISPs also provide other IT Services such as web hosting.
Invocation	(Service Design) Initiation of the steps defined in a plan. For example initiating the IT Service Continuity Plan for one or more IT Services.
Ishikawa Diagram	(Service Operation) (Continual Service Improvement) A technique that helps a team to identify all the possible causes of a Problem. Originally devised by Kaoru Ishikawa, the output of this technique is a diagram that looks like a fishbone.
ISO 9000	A generic term that refers to a number of international Standards and Guidelines for Quality Management Systems. See http://www.iso.org/ for more information. See ISO.
ISO 9001	An international Standard for Quality Management Systems. See ISO 9000, Standard.
ISO/IEC 17799	(Continual Service Improvement) ISO Code of Practice for Information Security Management. See Standard.
ISO/IEC 20000	ISO Specification and Code of Practice for IT Service Management. ISO/IEC 20000 is aligned with ITIL Best Practice.
ISO/IEC 27001	(Service Design) (Continual Service Improvement) ISO Specification for Information Security Management. The corresponding Code of Practice is ISO/IEC 17799. See Standard.
IT Directorate	(Continual Service Improvement) Senior Management within a Service Provider, charged with developing and delivering IT services. Most commonly used in UK Government departments.
IT Infrastructure	All of the hardware, software, networks, facilities etc. that are required to Develop, Test, deliver, Monitor, Control or support IT Services. The term IT Infrastructure includes all of the Information Technology but not the associated people, Processes and documentation.

IT Operations	(Service Operation) Activities carried out by IT Operations Control, including Console Management, Job Scheduling, Backup and Restore, and Print and Output Management. IT Operations is also used as a synonym for Service Operation.
IT Operations Control	(Service Operation) The Function responsible for Monitoring and Control of the IT Services and IT Infrastructure. See Operations Bridge.
IT Operations Management	(Service Operation) The Function within an IT Service Provider which performs the daily Activities needed to manage IT Services and the supporting IT Infrastructure. IT Operations Management includes IT Operations Control and Facilities Management.
IT Service	A Service provided to one or more Customers by an IT Service Provider. An IT Service is based on the use of Information Technology and supports the Customer's Business Processes. An IT Service is made up from a combination of people, Processes and technology and should be defined in a Service Level Agreement.
IT Service Continuity Management (ITSCM)	(Service Design) The Process responsible for managing Risks that could seriously impact IT Services. ITSCM ensures that the IT Service Provider can always provide minimum agreed Service Levels, by reducing the Risk to an acceptable level and Planning for the Recovery of IT Services. ITSCM should be designed to support Business Continuity Management.
IT Service Continuity Plan	(Service Design) A Plan defining the steps required to Recover one or more IT Services. The Plan will also identify the triggers for Invocation, people to be involved, communications etc. The IT Service Continuity Plan should be part of a Business Continuity Plan.
IT Service Management (ITSM)	The implementation and management of Quality IT Services that meet the needs of the Business. IT Service Management is performed by IT Service Providers through an appropriate mix of people, Process and Information Technology. See Service Management.
IT Service Management Forum (itSMF)	The IT Service Management Forum is an independent Organization dedicated to promoting a professional approach to IT Service Management. The itSMF is a not-for-profit membership Organization with representation in many countries around the world (itSMF Chapters). The itSMF and its membership contribute to the development of ITIL and associated IT Service Management Standards. See http://www.itsmf.com/ for more information.
IT Service Provider	(Service Strategy) A Service Provider that provides IT Services to Internal Customers or External Customers.
IT Steering Group (ISG)	A formal group that is responsible for ensuring that Business and IT Service Provider Strategies and Plans are closely aligned. An IT Steering Group includes senior representatives from the Business and the IT Service Provider.

ITIL	A set of Best Practice guidance for IT Service Management. ITIL is owned by the OGC and consists of a series of publications giving guidance on the provision of Quality IT Services, and on the Processes and facilities needed to support them. See http://www.itil.co.uk/ for more information.
Job Description	A Document which defines the Roles, responsibilities, skills and knowledge required by a particular person. One Job Description can include multiple Roles, for example the Roles of Configuration Manager and Change Manager may be carried out by one person.
Job Scheduling	(Service Operation) Planning and managing the execution of software tasks that are required as part of an IT Service. Job Scheduling is carried out by IT Operations Management, and is often automated using software tools that run batch or online tasks at specific times of the day, week, month or year.
Kano Model	(Service Strategy) A Model developed by Noriaki Kano that is used to help understand Customer preferences. The Kano Model considers Attributes of an IT Service grouped into areas such as Basic Factors, Excitement Factors, Performance Factors etc.
Kepner & Tregoe Analysis	(Service Operation) (Continual Service Improvement) A structured approach to Problem solving. The Problem is analyzed in terms of what, where, when and extent. Possible causes are identified. The most probable cause is tested. The true cause is verified.
Key Performance Indicator (KPI)	(Continual Service Improvement) A Metric that is used to help manage a Process, IT Service or Activity. Many Metrics may be measured, but only the most important of these are defined as KPIs and used to actively manage and report on the Process, IT Service or Activity. KPIs should be selected to ensure that Efficiency, Effectiveness, and Cost Effectiveness are all managed. See Critical Success Factor.
Knowledge Base	(Service Transition) A logical database containing the data used by the Service Knowledge Management System.
Knowledge Management	(Service Transition) The Process responsible for gathering, analyzing, storing and sharing knowledge and information within an Organization. The primary purpose of Knowledge Management is to improve Efficiency by reducing the need to rediscover knowledge. See Data-to-Information-to-Knowledge-to-Wisdom, Service Knowledge Management System.
Known Error	(Service Operation) A Problem that has a documented Root Cause and a Workaround. Known Errors are created and managed throughout their Lifecycle by Problem Management. Known Errors may also be identified by Development or Suppliers.
Known Error Database (KEDB)	(Service Operation) A database containing all Known Error Records. This database is created by Problem Management and used by Incident and Problem Management. The Known Error Database is part of the Service Knowledge Management System.

Known Error Record   (Service Operation) A Record containing the details of a Known Error. Each
                       Known Error Record documents the Lifecycle of a Known Error, including the
                       Status, Root Cause and Workaround. In some implementations a Known Error is
                       documented using additional fields in a Problem Record.

Lifecycle   The various stages in the life of an IT Service, Configuration Item, Incident,
                       Problem, Change etc. The Lifecycle defines the Categories for Status and the
                       Status transitions that are permitted. For example:
                       •   The Lifecycle of an Application includes Requirements, Design, Build, Deploy,
                           Operate, Optimize.
                       •   The Expanded Incident Lifecycle includes Detect, Respond, Diagnose, Repair,
                           Recover, Restore.
                       •   The lifecycle of a Server may include: Ordered, Received, In Test, Live,
                           Disposed etc.

Line of Service (LOS) (Service Strategy) A Core Service or Supporting Service that has multiple Service
                       Level Packages. A line of Service is managed by a Product Manager and each
                       Service Level Package is designed to support a particular market segment.

Live   (Service Transition) Refers to an IT Service or Configuration Item that is being
                       used to deliver Service to a Customer.

Live Environment   (Service Transition) A controlled Environment containing Live Configuration
                       Items used to deliver IT Services to Customers.

Maintainability   (Service Design) A measure of how quickly and Effectively a Configuration Item
                       or IT Service can be restored to normal working after a Failure. Maintainability is
                       often measured and reported as MTRS.
                       Maintainability is also used in the context of Software or IT Service Development
                       to mean ability to be Changed or Repaired easily.

Major Incident   (Service Operation) The highest Category of Impact for an Incident. A Major
                       Incident results in significant disruption to the Business.

Managed Services   (Service Strategy) A perspective on IT Services which emphasizes the fact that
                       they are managed. The term Managed Services is also used as a synonym for
                       Outsourced IT Services.

Management   Information that is used to support decision making by managers. Management
Information   Information is often generated automatically by tools supporting the various IT
                       Service Management Processes. Management Information often includes the
                       values of KPIs such as "Percentage of Changes leading to Incidents", or "first time
                       fix rate".

Management of Risk   The OGC methodology for managing Risks. MoR includes all the Activities
(MoR)   required to identify and Control the exposure to Risk which may have an impact
                       on the achievement of an Organization's Business Objectives.
                       See http://www.m-o-r.org/ for more details.

Management System   The framework of Policy, Processes and Functions that ensures an Organization
                       can achieve its Objectives.

Manual Workaround	A Workaround that requires manual intervention. Manual Workaround is also used as the name of a Recovery Option in which The Business Process Operates without the use of IT Services. This is a temporary measure and is usually combined with another Recovery Option.
Marginal Cost	(Service Strategy) The Cost of continuing to provide the IT Service. Marginal Cost does not include investment already made, for example the cost of developing new software and delivering training.
Market Space	(Service Strategy) All opportunities that an IT Service Provider could exploit to meet business needs of Customers. The Market Space identifies the possible IT Services that an IT Service Provider may wish to consider delivering.
Maturity	(Continual Service Improvement) A measure of the Reliability, Efficiency and Effectiveness of a Process, Function, Organization etc. The most mature Processes and Functions are formally aligned to Business Objectives and Strategy, and are supported by a framework for continual improvement.
Maturity Level	A named level in a Maturity model such as the Carnegie Mellon Capability Maturity Model Integration.
Mean Time Between Failures (MTBF)	(Service Design) A Metric for measuring and reporting Reliability. MTBF is the average time that a Configuration Item or IT Service can perform its agreed Function without interruption. This is measured from when the CI or IT Service starts working, until it next fails.
Mean Time Between Service Incidents (MTBSI)	(Service Design) A Metric used for measuring and reporting Reliability. MTBSI is the mean time from when a System or IT Service fails, until it next fails. MTBSI is equal to MTBF + MTRS.
Mean Time To Repair (MTTR)	The average time taken to repair a Configuration Item or IT Service after a Failure. MTTR is measured from when the CI or IT Service fails until it is Repaired. MTTR does not include the time required to Recover or Restore. MTTR is sometimes incorrectly used to mean Mean Time to Restore Service.
Mean Time to Restore Service (MTRS)	The average time taken to Restore a Configuration Item or IT Service after a Failure. MTRS is measured from when the CI or IT Service fails until it is fully Restored and delivering its normal functionality. See Maintainability, Mean Time to Repair.
Metric	(Continual Service Improvement) Something that is measured and reported to help manage a Process, IT Service or Activity. See KPI.
Middleware	(Service Design) Software that connects two or more software Components or Applications. Middleware is usually purchased from a Supplier, rather than developed within the IT Service Provider. See Off the Shelf.
Mission Statement	The Mission Statement of an Organization is a short but complete description of the overall purpose and intentions of that Organization. It states what is to be achieved, but not how this should be done.

Model	A representation of a System, Process, IT Service, Configuration Item etc. that is used to help understand or predict future behavior.
Modeling	A technique that is used to predict the future behavior of a System, Process, IT Service, Configuration Item etc. Modeling is commonly used in Financial Management, Capacity Management and Availability Management.
Monitor Control Loop	(Service Operation) Monitoring the output of a Task, Process, IT Service or Configuration Item; comparing this output to a predefined norm; and taking appropriate action based on this comparison.
Monitoring	(Service Operation) Repeated observation of a Configuration Item, IT Service or Process to detect Events and to ensure that the current status is known.
Near-Shore	(Service Strategy) Provision of Services from a country near the country where the Customer is based. This can be the provision of an IT Service, or of supporting Functions such as Service Desk. See On-shore, Off-shore.
Net Present Value (NPV)	(Service Strategy) A technique used to help make decisions about Capital Expenditure. NPV compares cash inflows to cash outflows. Positive NPV indicates that an investment is worthwhile. See Internal Rate of Return, Return on Investment.
Notional Charging	(Service Strategy) An approach to Charging for IT Services. Charges to Customers are calculated and Customers are informed of the charge, but no money is actually transferred. Notional Charging is sometimes introduced to ensure that Customers are aware of the Costs they incur, or as a stage during the introduction of real Charging.
Objective	The defined purpose or aim of a Process, an Activity or an Organization as a whole. Objectives are usually expressed as measurable targets. The term Objective is also informally used to mean a Requirement. See Outcome.
Off the Shelf	Synonym for Commercial Off the Shelf.
Office of Government Commerce (OGC)	OGC owns the ITIL brand (copyright and trademark). OGC is a UK Government department that supports the delivery of the government's procurement agenda through its work in collaborative procurement and in raising levels of procurement skills and capability with departments. It also provides support for complex public sector projects.
Office of Public Sector Information (OPSI)	OPSI license the Crown Copyright material used in the ITIL publications. They are a UK Government department who provide online access to UK legislation, license the re-use of Crown copyright material, manage the Information Fair Trader Scheme, maintain the Government's Information Asset Register and provide advice and guidance on official publishing and Crown copyright.

Off-shore	(Service Strategy) Provision of Services from a location outside the country where the Customer is based, often in a different continent. This can be the provision of an IT Service, or of supporting Functions such as Service Desk. See On-shore, Near-shore.
On-shore	(Service Strategy) Provision of Services from a location within the country where the Customer is based. See Off-shore, Near-shore.
Operate	To perform as expected. A Process or Configuration Item is said to Operate if it is delivering the Required outputs. Operate also means to perform one or more Operations. For example, to Operate a computer is to do the day-to-day Operations needed for it to perform as expected.
Operation	(Service Operation) Day-to-day management of an IT Service, System, or other Configuration Item. Operation is also used to mean any pre-defined Activity or Transaction. For example loading a magnetic tape, accepting money at a point of sale, or reading data from a disk drive.
Operational	The lowest of three levels of Planning and delivery (Strategic, Tactical, Operational). Operational Activities include the day-to-day or short term Planning or delivery of a Business Process or IT Service Management Process. The term Operational is also a synonym for Live.
Operational Cost	Cost resulting from running the IT Services. Often repeating payments. For example staff costs, hardware maintenance and electricity (also known as "current expenditure" or "revenue expenditure"). See Capital Expenditure.
Operational Expenditure (OPEX)	Synonym for Operational Cost.
Operational Level Agreement (OLA)	(Service Design) (Continual Service Improvement) An Agreement between an IT Service Provider and another part of the same Organization. An OLA supports the IT Service Provider's delivery of IT Services to Customers. The OLA defines the goods or Services to be provided and the responsibilities of both parties. For example there could be an OLA • between the IT Service Provider and a procurement department to obtain hardware in agreed times • between the Service Desk and a Support Group to provide Incident Resolution in agreed times. See Service Level Agreement.
Operations Bridge	(Service Operation) A physical location where IT Services and IT Infrastructure are monitored and managed.
Operations Control	Synonym for IT Operations Control.
Operations Management	Synonym for IT Operations Management.

Opportunity Cost	(Service Strategy) A Cost that is used in deciding between investment choices. Opportunity Cost represents the revenue that would have been generated by using the Resources in a different way. For example the Opportunity Cost of purchasing a new Server may include not carrying out a Service Improvement activity that the money could have been spent on. Opportunity cost analysis is used as part of a decision making processes, but is not treated as an actual Cost in any financial statement.
Optimize	Review, Plan and request Changes, in order to obtain the maximum Efficiency and Effectiveness from a Process, Configuration Item, Application etc.
Organization	A company, legal entity or other institution. Examples of Organizations that are not companies include International Standards Organization or itSMF. The term Organization is sometimes used to refer to any entity which has People, Resources and Budgets. For example a Project or Business Unit.
Outcome	The result of carrying out an Activity; following a Process; delivering an IT Service etc. The term Outcome is used to refer to intended results, as well as to actual results. See Objective.
Outsourcing	(Service Strategy) Using an External Service Provider to manage IT Services. See Service Sourcing, Type III Service Provider.
Overhead	Synonym for Indirect cost
Pain Value Analysis	(Service Operation) A technique used to help identify the Business Impact of one or more Problems. A formula is used to calculate Pain Value based on the number of Users affected, the duration of the Downtime, the Impact on each User, and the cost to the Business (if known).
Pareto Principle	(Service Operation) A technique used to priorities Activities. The Pareto Principle says that 80% of the value of any Activity is created with 20% of the effort. Pareto Analysis is also used in Problem Management to priorities possible Problem causes for investigation.
Partnership	A relationship between two Organizations which involves working closely together for common goals or mutual benefit. The IT Service Provider should have a Partnership with the Business, and with Third Parties who are critical to the delivery of IT Services. See Value Network.
Passive Monitoring	(Service Operation) Monitoring of a Configuration Item, an IT Service or a Process that relies on an Alert or notification to discover the current status. See Active Monitoring.
Pattern of Business Activity (PBA)	(Service Strategy) A Workload profile of one or more Business Activities. Patterns of Business Activity are used to help the IT Service Provider understand and plan for different levels of Business Activity. See User Profile.

Percentage utilization	(Service Design) The amount of time that a Component is busy over a given period of time. For example, if a CPU is busy for 1800 seconds in a one hour period, its utilization is 50%
Performance	A measure of what is achieved or delivered by a System, person, team, Process, or IT Service.
Performance Anatomy	(Service Strategy) An approach to Organizational Culture that integrates, and actively manages, leadership and strategy, people development, technology enablement, performance management and innovation.
Performance Management	(Continual Service Improvement) The Process responsible for day-to-day Capacity Management Activities. These include Monitoring, Threshold detection, Performance analysis and Tuning, and implementing Changes related to Performance and Capacity.
Pilot	(Service Transition) A limited Deployment of an IT Service, a Release or a Process to the Live Environment. A Pilot is used to reduce Risk and to gain User feedback and Acceptance. See Test, Evaluation.
Plan	A detailed proposal which describes the Activities and Resources needed to achieve an Objective. For example a Plan to implement a new IT Service or Process. ISO/IEC 20000 requires a Plan for the management of each IT Service Management Process.
Plan-Do-Check-Act	(Continual Service Improvement) A four stage cycle for Process management, attributed to Edward Deming. Plan-Do-Check-Act is also called the Deming Cycle. PLAN: Design or revise Processes that support the IT Services. DO: Implement the Plan and manage the Processes. CHECK: Measure the Processes and IT Services, compare with Objectives and produce reports ACT: Plan and implement Changes to improve the Processes.
Planned Downtime	(Service Design) Agreed time when an IT Service will not be available. Planned Downtime is often used for maintenance, upgrades and testing. See Change Window, Downtime.
Planning	An Activity responsible for creating one or more Plans. For example, Capacity Planning.
PMBOK	A Project management Standard maintained and published by the Project Management Institute. PMBOK stands for Project Management Body of Knowledge. See http://www.pmi.org/ for more information. See PRINCE2.
Policy	Formally documented management expectations and intentions. Policies are used to direct decisions, and to ensure consistent and appropriate development and implementation of Processes, Standards, Roles, Activities, IT Infrastructure etc.

Portable Facility	(Service Design) A prefabricated building, or a large vehicle, provided by a Third Party and moved to a site when needed by an IT Service Continuity Plan. See Recovery Option, Fixed Facility.
Post Implementation Review (PIR)	A Review that takes place after a Change or a Project has been implemented. A PIR determines if the Change or Project was successful, and identifies opportunities for improvement.
Practice	A way of working, or a way in which work must be done. Practices can include Activities, Processes, Functions, Standards and Guidelines. See Best Practice.
Prerequisite for Success (PFS)	An Activity that needs to be completed, or a condition that needs to be met, to enable successful implementation of a Plan or Process. A PFS is often an output from one Process that is a required input to another Process.
Pricing	(Service Strategy) The Activity for establishing how much Customers will be Charged.
PRINCE2	The standard UK government methodology for Project management. See http://www.ogc.gov.uk/prince2/ for more information. See PMBOK.
Priority	(Service Transition) (Service Operation) A Category used to identify the relative importance of an Incident, Problem or Change. Priority is based on Impact and Urgency, and is used to identify required times for actions to be taken. For example the SLA may state that Priority2 Incidents must be resolved within 12 hours.
Proactive Monitoring	(Service Operation) Monitoring that looks for patterns of Events to predict possible future Failures. See Reactive Monitoring.
Proactive Problem Management	(Service Operation) Part of the Problem Management Process. The Objective of Proactive Problem Management is to identify Problems that might otherwise be missed. Proactive Problem Management analyses Incident Records, and uses data collected by other IT Service Management Processes to identify trends or significant Problems.
Problem	(Service Operation) A cause of one or more Incidents. The cause is not usually known at the time a Problem Record is created, and the Problem Management Process is responsible for further investigation.
Problem Management	(Service Operation) The Process responsible for managing the Lifecycle of all Problems. The primary Objectives of Problem Management are to prevent Incidents from happening, and to minimize the Impact of Incidents that cannot be prevented.
Problem Record	(Service Operation) A Record containing the details of a Problem. Each Problem Record documents the Lifecycle of a single Problem.

Procedure	A Document containing steps that specify how to achieve an Activity. Procedures are defined as part of Processes. See Work Instruction.
Process	A structured set of Activities designed to accomplish a specific Objective. A Process takes one or more defined inputs and turns them into defined outputs. A Process may include any of the Roles, responsibilities, tools and management Controls required to reliably deliver the outputs. A Process may define Policies, Standards, Guidelines, Activities, and Work Instructions if they are needed.
Process Control	The Activity of planning and regulating a Process, with the Objective of performing the Process in an Effective, Efficient, and consistent manner.
Process Manager	A Role responsible for Operational management of a Process. The Process Manager's responsibilities include Planning and coordination of all Activities required to carry out, monitor and report on the Process. There may be several Process Managers for one Process, for example regional Change Managers or IT Service Continuity Managers for each data centre. The Process Manager Role is often assigned to the person who carries out the Process Owner Role, but the two Roles may be separate in larger Organizations.
Process Owner	A Role responsible for ensuring that a Process is Fit for Purpose. The Process Owner's responsibilities include sponsorship, Design, Change Management and continual improvement of the Process and its Metrics. This Role is often assigned to the same person who carries out the Process Manager Role, but the two Roles may be separate in larger Organizations.
Production Environment	Synonym for Live Environment.
Profit Centre	(Service Strategy) A Business Unit which charges for Services provided. A Profit Centre can be created with the objective of making a profit, recovering Costs, or running at a loss. An IT Service Provider can be run as a Cost Centre or a Profit Centre.
pro-forma	A template, or example Document containing example data that will be replaced with the real values when these are available.
Program	A number of Projects and Activities that are planned and managed together to achieve an overall set of related Objectives and other Outcomes.
Project	A temporary Organization, with people and other Assets required to achieve an Objective or other Outcome. Each Project has a Lifecycle that typically includes initiation, Planning, execution, Closure etc. Projects are usually managed using a formal methodology such as PRINCE2.
Projected Service Outage (PSO)	(Service Transition) A Document that identifies the effect of planned Changes, maintenance Activities and Test Plans on agreed Service Levels.

PRojects IN Controlled Environments (PRINCE2)	See PRINCE2
Qualification	(Service Transition) An Activity that ensures that IT Infrastructure is appropriate, and correctly configured, to support an Application or IT Service. See Validation.
Quality	The ability of a product, Service, or Process to provide the intended value. For example, a hardware Component can be considered to be of high Quality if it performs as expected and delivers the required Reliability. Process Quality also requires an ability to monitor Effectiveness and Efficiency, and to improve them if necessary. See Quality Management System.
Quality Assurance (QA)	(Service Transition) The Process responsible for ensuring that the Quality of a product, Service or Process will provide its intended Value.
Quality Management System (QMS)	(Continual Service Improvement) The set of Processes responsible for ensuring that all work carried out by an Organization is of a suitable Quality to reliably meet Business Objectives or Service Levels. See ISO 9000.
Quick Win	(Continual Service Improvement) An improvement Activity which is expected to provide a Return on Investment in a short period of time with relatively small Cost and effort. See Pareto Principle.
RACI	(Service Design) (Continual Service Improvement) A Model used to help define Roles and Responsibilities. RACI stands for Responsible, Accountable, Consulted and Informed. See Stakeholder.
Reactive Monitoring	(Service Operation) Monitoring that takes action in response to an Event. For example submitting a batch job when the previous job completes, or logging an Incident when an Error occurs. See Proactive Monitoring.
Reciprocal Arrangement	(Service Design) A Recovery Option. An agreement between two Organizations to share resources in an emergency. For example, Computer Room space or use of a mainframe.
Record	A Document containing the results or other output from a Process or Activity. Records are evidence of the fact that an Activity took place and may be paper or electronic. For example, an Audit report, an Incident Record, or the minutes of a meeting.

Recovery	(Service Design) (Service Operation) Returning a Configuration Item or an IT Service to a working state. Recovery of an IT Service often includes recovering data to a known consistent state. After Recovery, further steps may be needed before the IT Service can be made available to the Users (Restoration).
Recovery Option	(Service Design) A Strategy for responding to an interruption to Service. Commonly used Strategies are Do Nothing, Manual Workaround, Reciprocal Arrangement, Gradual Recovery, Intermediate Recovery, Fast Recovery, Immediate Recovery. Recovery Options may make use of dedicated facilities, or Third Party facilities shared by multiple Businesses.
Recovery Point Objective (RPO)	(Service Operation) The maximum amount of data that may be lost when Service is Restored after an interruption. Recovery Point Objective is expressed as a length of time before the Failure. For example a Recovery Point Objective of one day may be supported by daily Backups, and up to 24 hours of data may be lost. Recovery Point Objectives for each IT Service should be negotiated, agreed and documented, and used as Requirements for Service Design and IT Service Continuity Plans.
Recovery Time Objective (RTO)	(Service Operation) The maximum time allowed for recovery of an IT Service following an interruption. The Service Level to be provided may be less than normal Service Level Targets. Recovery Time Objectives for each IT Service should be negotiated, agreed and documented. See Business Impact Analysis.
Redundancy	Synonym for Fault Tolerance. The term Redundant also has a generic meaning of obsolete, or no longer needed.
Relationship	A connection or interaction between two people or things. In Business Relationship Management it is the interaction between the IT Service Provider and the Business. In Configuration Management it is a link between two Configuration Items that identifies a dependency or connection between them. For example Applications may be linked to the Servers they run on, IT Services have many links to all the CIs that contribute to them.
Relationship Processes	The ISO/IEC 20000 Process group that includes Business Relationship Management and Supplier Management.
Release	(Service Transition) A collection of hardware, software, documentation, Processes or other Components required to implement one or more approved Changes to IT Services. The contents of each Release are managed, Tested, and Deployed as a single entity.
Release and Deployment Management	(Service Transition) The Process responsible for both Release Management and Deployment.
Release Identification	(Service Transition) A naming convention used to uniquely identify a Release. The Release Identification typically includes a reference to the Configuration Item and a version number. For example Microsoft Office 2003 SR2.

Release Management   (Service Transition) The Process responsible for Planning, scheduling and controlling the movement of Releases to Test and Live Environments. The primary Objective of Release Management is to ensure that the integrity of the Live Environment is protected and that the correct Components are released. Release Management is part of the Release and Deployment Management Process.

Release Process   The name used by ISO/IEC 20000 for the Process group that includes Release Management. This group does not include any other Processes.
Release Process is also used as a synonym for Release Management Process.

Release Record   (Service Transition) A Record in the CMDB that defines the content of a Release. A Release Record has Relationships with all Configuration Items that are affected by the Release.

Release Unit   (Service Transition) Components of an IT Service that are normally Released together. A Release Unit typically includes sufficient Components to perform a useful Function. For example one Release Unit could be a Desktop PC, including Hardware, Software, Licenses, Documentation etc. A different Release Unit may be the complete Payroll Application, including IT Operations Procedures and User training.

Release Window   Synonym for Change Window.

Reliability   (Service Design) (Continual Service Improvement) A measure of how long a Configuration Item or IT Service can perform its agreed Function without interruption. Usually measured as MTBF or MTBSI. The term Reliability can also be used to state how likely it is that a Process, Function etc. will deliver its required outputs.
See Availability.

Remediation   (Service Transition) Recovery to a known state after a failed Change or Release.

Repair   (Service Operation) The replacement or correction of a failed Configuration Item.

Request for Change (RFC)   (Service Transition) A formal proposal for a Change to be made. An RFC includes details of the proposed Change, and may be recorded on paper or electronically. The term RFC is often misused to mean a Change Record, or the Change itself.

Request Fulfilment   (Service Operation) The Process responsible for managing the Lifecycle of all Service Requests.

Requirement   (Service Design) A formal statement of what is needed. For example a Service Level Requirement, a Project Requirement or the required Deliverables for a Process.
See Statement of Requirements.

Resilience   (Service Design) The ability of a Configuration Item or IT Service to resist Failure or to Recover quickly following a Failure. For example, an armored cable will resist failure when put under stress.
See Fault Tolerance.

Resolution	(Service Operation) Action taken to repair the Root Cause of an Incident or Problem, or to implement a Workaround. In ISO/IEC 20000, Resolution Processes is the Process group that includes Incident and Problem Management.
Resolution Processes	The ISO/IEC 20000 Process group that includes Incident Management and Problem Management.
Resource	(Service Strategy) A generic term that includes IT Infrastructure, people, money or anything else that might help to deliver an IT Service. Resources are considered to be Assets of an Organization. See Capability, Service Asset.
Response Time	A measure of the time taken to complete an Operation or Transaction. Used in Capacity Management as a measure of IT Infrastructure Performance, and in Incident Management as a measure of the time taken to answer the phone, or to start Diagnosis.
Responsiveness	A measurement of the time taken to respond to something. This could be Response Time of a Transaction, or the speed with which an IT Service Provider responds to an Incident or Request for Change etc.
Restoration of Service	See Restore.
Restore	(Service Operation) Taking action to return an IT Service to the Users after Repair and Recovery from an Incident. This is the primary Objective of Incident Management.
Retire	(Service Transition) Permanent removal of an IT Service, or other Configuration Item, from the Live Environment. Retired is a stage in the Lifecycle of many Configuration Items.
Return on Investment (ROI)	(Service Strategy) (Continual Service Improvement) A measurement of the expected benefit of an investment. In the simplest sense it is the net profit of an investment divided by the net worth of the assets invested. See Net Present Value, Value on Investment.
Return to Normal	(Service Design) The phase of an IT Service Continuity Plan during which full normal operations are resumed. For example, if an alternate data centre has been in use, then this phase will bring the primary data centre back into operation, and restore the ability to invoke IT Service Continuity Plans again.
Review	An evaluation of a Change, Problem, Process, Project etc. Reviews are typically carried out at predefined points in the Lifecycle, and especially after Closure. The purpose of a Review is to ensure that all Deliverables have been provided, and to identify opportunities for improvement. See Post Implementation Review.
Rights	(Service Operation) Entitlements, or permissions, granted to a User or Role. For example the Right to modify particular data, or to authorize a Change.

Risk	A possible Event that could cause harm or loss, or affect the ability to achieve Objectives. A Risk is measured by the probability of a Threat, the Vulnerability of the Asset to that Threat, and the Impact it would have if it occurred.
Risk Assessment	The initial steps of Risk Management. Analyzing the value of Assets to the business, identifying Threats to those Assets, and evaluating how Vulnerable each Asset is to those Threats. Risk Assessment can be quantitative (based on numerical data) or qualitative.
Risk Management	The Process responsible for identifying, assessing and controlling Risks. See Risk Assessment.
Role	A set of responsibilities, Activities and authorities granted to a person or team. A Role is defined in a Process. One person or team may have multiple Roles, for example the Roles of Configuration Manager and Change Manager may be carried out by a single person.
Rollout	(Service Transition) Synonym for Deployment. Most often used to refer to complex or phased Deployments or Deployments to multiple locations.
Root Cause	(Service Operation) The underlying or original cause of an Incident or Problem.
Root Cause Analysis (RCA)	(Service Operation) An Activity that identifies the Root Cause of an Incident or Problem. RCA typically concentrates on IT Infrastructure failures. See Service Failure Analysis.
Running Costs	Synonym for Operational Costs
Scalability	The ability of an IT Service, Process, Configuration Item etc. to perform its agreed Function when the Workload or Scope changes.
Scope	The boundary, or extent, to which a Process, Procedure, Certification, Contract etc. applies. For example the Scope of Change Management may include all Live IT Services and related Configuration Items, the Scope of an ISO/IEC 20000 Certificate may include all IT Services delivered out of a named data centre.
Second-line Support	(Service Operation) The second level in a hierarchy of Support Groups involved in the resolution of Incidents and investigation of Problems. Each level contains more specialist skills, or has more time or other Resources.
Security	See Information Security Management
Security Management	Synonym for Information Security Management
Security Policy	Synonym for Information Security Policy
Separation of Concerns (SoC)	(Service Strategy) An approach to Designing a solution or IT Service that divides the problem into pieces that can be solved independently. This approach separates "what" is to be done from "how" it is to be done.
Server	(Service Operation) A computer that is connected to a network and provides software Functions that are used by other computers.

Service	A means of delivering value to Customers by facilitating Outcomes Customers want to achieve without the ownership of specific Costs and Risks.
Service Acceptance Criteria (SAC)	(Service Transition) A set of criteria used to ensure that an IT Service meets its functionality and Quality Requirements and that the IT Service Provider is ready to Operate the new IT Service when it has been Deployed. See Acceptance.
Service Analytics	(Service Strategy) A technique used in the Assessment of the Business Impact of Incidents. Service Analytics Models the dependencies between Configuration Items, and the dependencies of IT Services on Configuration Items.
Service Asset	Any Capability or Resource of a Service Provider. See Asset.
Service Asset and Configuration Management (SACM)	(Service Transition) The Process responsible for both Configuration Management and Asset Management.
Service Capacity Management (SCM)	(Service Design) (Continual Service Improvement) The Activity responsible for understanding the Performance and Capacity of IT Services. The Resources used by each IT Service and the pattern of usage over time are collected, recorded, and analyzed for use in the Capacity Plan. See Business Capacity Management, Component Capacity Management.
Service Catalogue	(Service Design) A database or structured Document with information about all Live IT Services, including those available for Deployment. The Service Catalogue is the only part of the Service Portfolio published to Customers, and is used to support the sale and delivery of IT Services. The Service Catalogue includes information about deliverables, prices, contact points, ordering and request Processes. See Contract Portfolio.
Service Continuity Management	Synonym for IT Service Continuity Management.
Service Contract	(Service Strategy) A Contract to deliver one or more IT Services. The term Service Contract is also used to mean any Agreement to deliver IT Services, whether this is a legal Contract or an SLA. See Contract Portfolio.
Service Culture	A Customer oriented Culture. The major Objectives of a Service Culture are Customer satisfaction and helping the Customer to achieve their Business Objectives.
Service Design	(Service Design) A stage in the Lifecycle of an IT Service. Service Design includes a number of Processes and Functions and is the title of one of the Core ITIL publications. See Design.

Service Design Package	(Service Design) Document(s) defining all aspects of an IT Service and its Requirements through each stage of its Lifecycle. A Service Design Package is produced for each new IT Service, major Change, or IT Service Retirement.
Service Desk	(Service Operation) The Single Point of Contact between the Service Provider and the Users. A typical Service Desk manages Incidents and Service Requests, and also handles communication with the Users.
Service Failure Analysis (SFA)	(Service Design) An Activity that identifies underlying causes of one or more IT Service interruptions. SFA identifies opportunities to improve the IT Service Provider's Processes and tools, and not just the IT Infrastructure. SFA is a time constrained, project-like activity, rather than an ongoing process of analysis. See Root Cause Analysis.
Service Hours	(Service Design) (Continual Service Improvement) An agreed time period when a particular IT Service should be Available. For example, "Monday-Friday 08:00 to 17:00 except public holidays". Service Hours should be defined in a Service Level Agreement.
Service Improvement Plan (SIP)	(Continual Service Improvement) A formal Plan to implement improvements to a Process or IT Service.
Service Knowledge Management System (SKMS)	(Service Transition) A set of tools and databases that are used to manage knowledge and information. The SKMS includes the Configuration Management System, as well as other tools and databases. The SKMS stores, manages, updates, and presents all information that an IT Service Provider needs to manage the full Lifecycle of IT Services.
Service Level	Measured and reported achievement against one or more Service Level Targets. The term Service Level is sometimes used informally to mean Service Level Target.
Service Level Agreement (SLA)	(Service Design) (Continual Service Improvement) An Agreement between an IT Service Provider and a Customer. The SLA describes the IT Service, documents Service Level Targets, and specifies the responsibilities of the IT Service Provider and the Customer. A single SLA may cover multiple IT Services or multiple Customers. See Operational Level Agreement.
Service Level Management (SLM)	(Service Design) (Continual Service Improvement) The Process responsible for negotiating Service Level Agreements, and ensuring that these are met. SLM is responsible for ensuring that all IT Service Management Processes, Operational Level Agreements, and Underpinning Contracts, are appropriate for the agreed Service Level Targets. SLM monitors and reports on Service Levels, and holds regular Customer reviews.
Service Level Package (SLP)	(Service Strategy) A defined level of Utility and Warranty for a particular Service Package. Each SLP is designed to meet the needs of a particular Pattern of Business Activity. See Line of Service.

Service Level Requirement (SLR)	(Service Design) (Continual Service Improvement) A Customer Requirement for an aspect of an IT Service. SLRs are based on Business Objectives and are used to negotiate agreed Service Level Targets.
Service Level Target	(Service Design) (Continual Service Improvement) A commitment that is documented in a Service Level Agreement. Service Level Targets are based on Service Level Requirements, and are needed to ensure that the IT Service design is Fit for Purpose. Service Level Targets should be SMART, and are usually based on KPIs.
Service Maintenance Objective	(Service Operation) The expected time that a Configuration Item will be unavailable due to planned maintenance Activity.
Service Management	Service Management is a set of specialized organizational capabilities for providing value to customers in the form of services.
Service Management Lifecycle	An approach to IT Service Management that emphasizes the importance of coordination and Control across the various Functions, Processes, and Systems necessary to manage the full Lifecycle of IT Services. The Service Management Lifecycle approach considers the Strategy, Design, Transition, Operation and Continuous Improvement of IT Services.
Service Manager	A manager who is responsible for managing the end-to-end Lifecycle of one or more IT Services. The term Service Manager is also used to mean any manager within the IT Service Provider. Most commonly used to refer to a Business Relationship Manager, a Process Manager, an Account Manager or a senior manager with responsibility for IT Services overall.
Service Operation	(Service Operation) A stage in the Lifecycle of an IT Service. Service Operation includes a number of Processes and Functions and is the title of one of the Core ITIL publications. See Operation.
Service Owner	(Continual Service Improvement) A Role which is accountable for the delivery of a specific IT Service.
Service Package	(Service Strategy) A detailed description of an IT Service that is available to be delivered to Customers. A Service Package includes a Service Level Package and one or more Core Services and Supporting Services.
Service Pipeline	(Service Strategy) A database or structured Document listing all IT Services that are under consideration or Development, but are not yet available to Customers. The Service Pipeline provides a Business view of possible future IT Services and is part of the Service Portfolio which is not normally published to Customers.
Service Portfolio	(Service Strategy) The complete set of Services that are managed by a Service Provider. The Service Portfolio is used to manage the entire Lifecycle of all Services, and includes three Categories: Service Pipeline (proposed or in Development); Service Catalogue (Live or available for Deployment); and Retired Services. See Service Portfolio Management, Contract Portfolio.

Service Portfolio
Management (SPM)

(Service Strategy) The Process responsible for managing the Service Portfolio.
Service Portfolio Management considers Services in terms of the Business value
that they provide.

Service Potential

(Service Strategy) The total possible value of the overall Capabilities and Resources
of the IT Service Provider.

Service Provider

(Service Strategy) An Organization supplying Services to one or more Internal
Customers or External Customers. Service Provider is often used as an
abbreviation for IT Service Provider.
See Type I Service Provider, Type II Service Provider, Type III Service Provider.

Service Provider
Interface (SPI)

(Service Strategy) An interface between the IT Service Provider and a User,
Customer, Business Process, or a Supplier. Analysis of Service Provider Interfaces
helps to coordinate end-to-end management of IT Services.

Service Provisioning
Optimization (SPO)

(Service Strategy) Analyzing the finances and constraints of an IT Service to
decide if alternative approaches to Service delivery might reduce Costs or improve
Quality.

Service Reporting

(Continual Service Improvement) The Process responsible for producing and
delivering reports of achievement and trends against Service Levels. Service
Reporting should agree the format, content and frequency of reports with
Customers.

Service Request

(Service Operation) A request from a User for information, or advice, or for a
Standard Change or for Access to an IT Service. For example to reset a password,
or to provide standard IT Services for a new User. Service Requests are usually
handled by a Service Desk, and do not require an RFC to be submitted.
See Request Fulfilment.

Service Sourcing

(Service Strategy) The Strategy and approach for deciding whether to provide
a Service internally or to Outsource it to an External Service Provider. Service
Sourcing also means the execution of this Strategy.
Service Sourcing includes:
• Internal Sourcing - Internal or Shared Services using Type I or Type II Service
  Providers.
• Traditional Sourcing - Full Service Outsourcing using a Type III Service
  Provider.
• Multivendor Sourcing - Prime, Consortium or Selective Outsourcing using
  Type III Service Providers.

Service Strategy

(Service Strategy) The title of one of the Core ITIL publications. Service Strategy
establishes an overall Strategy for IT Services and for IT Service Management.

Service Transition

(Service Transition) A stage in the Lifecycle of an IT Service. Service Transition
includes a number of Processes and Functions and is the title of one of the Core
ITIL publications.
See Transition.

Service Utility	(Service Strategy) The Functionality of an IT Service from the Customer's perspective. The Business value of an IT Service is created by the combination of Service Utility (what the Service does) and Service Warranty (how well it does it). See Utility.
Service Validation and Testing	(Service Transition) The Process responsible for Validation and Testing of a new or Changed IT Service. Service Validation and Testing ensures that the IT Service matches its Design Specification and will meet the needs of the Business.
Service Valuation	(Service Strategy) A measurement of the total Cost of delivering an IT Service, and the total value to the Business of that IT Service. Service Valuation is used to help the Business and the IT Service Provider agree on the value of the IT Service.
Service Warranty	(Service Strategy) Assurance that an IT Service will meet agreed Requirements. This may be a formal Agreement such as a Service Level Agreement or Contract, or may be a marketing message or brand image. The Business value of an IT Service is created by the combination of Service Utility (what the Service does) and Service Warranty (how well it does it). See Warranty.
Serviceability	(Service Design) (Continual Service Improvement) The ability of a Third Party Supplier to meet the terms of their Contract. This Contract will include agreed levels of Reliability, Maintainability or Availability for a Configuration Item.
Shift	(Service Operation) A group or team of people who carry out a specific Role for a fixed period of time. For example there could be four shifts of IT Operations Control personnel to support an IT Service that is used 24 hours a day.
Simulation modeling	(Service Design) (Continual Service Improvement) A technique that creates a detailed Model to predict the behavior of a Configuration Item or IT Service. Simulation Models can be very accurate but are expensive and time consuming to create. A Simulation Model is often created by using the actual Configuration Items that are being modeled, with artificial Workloads or Transactions. They are used in Capacity Management when accurate results are important. A simulation model is sometimes called a Performance Benchmark.
Single Point of Contact	(Service Operation) Providing a single consistent way to communicate with an Organization or Business Unit. For example, a Single Point of Contact for an IT Service Provider is usually called a Service Desk.
Single Point of Failure (SPOF)	(Service Design) Any Configuration Item that can cause an Incident when it fails, and for which a Countermeasure has not been implemented. A SPOF may be a person, or a step in a Process or Activity, as well as a Component of the IT Infrastructure. See Failure.
SLAM Chart	(Continual Service Improvement) A Service Level Agreement Monitoring Chart is used to help monitor and report achievements against Service Level Targets. A SLAM Chart is typically color coded to show whether each agreed Service Level Target has been met, missed, or nearly missed during each of the previous 12 months.

SMART	(Service Design) (Continual Service Improvement) An acronym for helping to remember that targets in Service Level Agreements and Project Plans should be Specific, Measurable, Achievable, Relevant and Timely.
Snapshot	(Service Transition) The current state of a Configuration as captured by a discovery tool. Also used as a synonym for Benchmark. See Baseline.
Source	See Service Sourcing.
Specification	A formal definition of Requirements. A Specification may be used to define technical or Operational Requirements, and may be internal or external. Many public Standards consist of a Code of Practice and a Specification. The Specification defines the Standard against which an Organization can be Audited.
Stakeholder	All people who have an interest in an Organization, Project, IT Service etc. Stakeholders may be interested in the Activities, targets, Resources, or Deliverables. Stakeholders may include Customers, Partners, employees, shareholders, owners, etc. See RACI.
Standard	A mandatory Requirement. Examples include ISO/IEC 20000 (an international Standard), an internal security Standard for Unix configuration, or a government Standard for how financial Records should be maintained. The term Standard is also used to refer to a Code of Practice or Specification published by a Standards Organization such as ISO or BSI. See Guideline.
Standard Change	(Service Transition) A pre-approved Change that is low Risk, relatively common and follows a Procedure or Work Instruction. For example password reset or provision of standard equipment to a new employee. RFCs are not required to implement a Standard Change, and they are logged and tracked using a different mechanism, such as a Service Request. See Change Model.
Standard Operating Procedures (SOP)	(Service Operation) Procedures used by IT Operations Management.
Standby	(Service Design) Used to refer to Resources that are not required to deliver the Live IT Services, but are available to support IT Service Continuity Plans. For example a Standby data centre may be maintained to support Hot Standby, Warm Standby or Cold Standby arrangements.
Statement of requirements (SOR)	(Service Design) A Document containing all Requirements for a product purchase, or a new or changed IT Service. See Terms of Reference.
Status	The name of a required field in many types of Record. It shows the current stage in the Lifecycle of the associated Configuration Item, Incident, Problem etc.

Status Accounting   (Service Transition) The Activity responsible for recording and reporting the
                       Lifecycle of each Configuration Item.

Storage Management   (Service Operation) The Process responsible for managing the storage and
                       maintenance of data throughout its Lifecycle.

Strategic   (Service Strategy) The highest of three levels of Planning and delivery (Strategic,
                       Tactical, Operational). Strategic Activities include Objective setting and long term
                       Planning to achieve the overall Vision.

Strategy   (Service Strategy) A Strategic Plan designed to achieve defined Objectives.

Super User   (Service Operation) A User who helps other Users, and assists in communication
                       with the Service Desk or other parts of the IT Service Provider. Super Users
                       typically provide support for minor Incidents and training.

Supplier   (Service Strategy) (Service Design) A Third Party responsible for supplying goods
                       or Services that are required to deliver IT services. Examples of suppliers include
                       commodity hardware and software vendors, network and telecom providers, and
                       Outsourcing Organizations.
                       See Underpinning Contract, Supply Chain.

Supplier and   (Service Design) A database or structured Document used to manage Supplier
Contract Database   Contracts throughout their Lifecycle. The SCD contains key Attributes of
(SCD)   all Contracts with Suppliers, and should be part of the Service Knowledge
                       Management System.

Supplier   (Service Design) The Process responsible for ensuring that all Contracts with
Management   Suppliers support the needs of the Business, and that all Suppliers meet their
                       contractual commitments.

Supply Chain   (Service Strategy) The Activities in a Value Chain carried out by Suppliers. A
                       Supply Chain typically involves multiple Suppliers, each adding value to the
                       product or Service.
                       See Value Network.

Support Group   (Service Operation) A group of people with technical skills. Support Groups
                       provide the Technical Support needed by all of the IT Service Management
                       Processes.
                       See Technical Management.

Support Hours   (Service Design) (Service Operation) The times or hours when support is available
                       to the Users. Typically this is the hours when the Service Desk is available. Support
                       Hours should be defined in a Service Level Agreement, and may be different from
                       Service Hours. For example, Service Hours may be 24 hours a day, but the Support
                       Hours may be 07:00 to 19:00.

Supporting Service   (Service Strategy) A Service that enables or enhances a Core Service. For example
                       a Directory Service or a Backup Service.
                       See Service Package.

SWOT Analysis	(Continual Service Improvement) A technique that reviews and analyses the internal strengths and weaknesses of an Organization and the external opportunities and threats which it faces SWOT stands for Strengths, Weaknesses, Opportunities and Threats.
System	A number of related things that work together to achieve an overall Objective. For example: • A computer System including hardware, software and Applications. • A management System, including multiple Processes that are planned and managed together. For example a Quality Management System. • A Database Management System or Operating System that includes many software modules that are designed to perform a set of related Functions.
System Management	The part of IT Service Management that focuses on the management of IT Infrastructure rather than Process.
Tactical	The middle of three levels of Planning and delivery (Strategic, Tactical, Operational). Tactical Activities include the medium term Plans required to achieve specific Objectives, typically over a period of weeks to months.
Tag	(Service Strategy) A short code used to identify a Category. For example tags EC1, EC2, EC3 etc. might be used to identify different Customer outcomes when analyzing and comparing Strategies. The term Tag is also used to refer to the Activity of assigning Tags to things.
Technical Management	(Service Operation) The Function responsible for providing technical skills in support of IT Services and management of the IT Infrastructure. Technical Management defines the Roles of Support Groups, as well as the tools, Processes and Procedures required.
Technical Observation (TO)	(Continual Service Improvement) A technique used in Service Improvement, Problem investigation and Availability Management. Technical support staff meet to monitor the behavior and Performance of an IT Service and make recommendations for improvement.
Technical Service	Synonym for Infrastructure Service.
Technical Support	Synonym for Technical Management.
Tension Metrics	(Continual Service Improvement) A set of related Metrics, in which improvements to one Metric have a negative effect on another. Tension Metrics are designed to ensure that an appropriate balance is achieved.
Terms of Reference (TOR)	(Service Design) A Document specifying the Requirements, Scope, Deliverables, Resources and schedule for a Project or Activity.
Test	(Service Transition) An Activity that verifies that a Configuration Item, IT Service, Process, etc. meets its Specification or agreed Requirements. See Service Validation and Testing, Acceptance.
Test Environment	(Service Transition) A controlled Environment used to Test Configuration Items, Builds, IT Services, Processes etc.

Third Party	A person, group, or Business who is not part of the Service Level Agreement for an IT Service, but is required to ensure successful delivery of that IT Service. For example a software Supplier, a hardware maintenance company, or a facilities department. Requirements for Third Parties are typically specified in Underpinning Contracts or Operational Level Agreements.
Third-line Support	(Service Operation) The third level in a hierarchy of Support Groups involved in the resolution of Incidents and investigation of Problems. Each level contains more specialist skills, or has more time or other Resources.
Threat	Anything that might exploit a Vulnerability. Any potential cause of an Incident can be considered to be a Threat. For example a fire is a Threat that could exploit the Vulnerability of flammable floor coverings. This term is commonly used in Information Security Management and IT Service Continuity Management, but also applies to other areas such as Problem and Availability Management.
Threshold	The value of a Metric which should cause an Alert to be generated, or management action to be taken. For example "Priority1 Incident not solved within 4 hours", "more than 5 soft disk errors in an hour", or "more than 10 failed changes in a month".
Throughput	(Service Design) A measure of the number of Transactions, or other Operations, performed in a fixed time. For example 5000 emails sent per hour, or 200 disk I/Os per second.
Total Cost of Ownership (TCO)	(Service Strategy) A methodology used to help make investment decisions. TCO assesses the full Lifecycle Cost of owning a Configuration Item, not just the initial Cost or purchase price. See Total Cost of Utilization.
Total Cost of Utilization (TCU)	(Service Strategy) A methodology used to help make investment and Service Sourcing decisions. TCU assesses the full Lifecycle Cost to the Customer of using an IT Service. See Total Cost of Ownership.
Total Quality Management (TQM)	(Continual Service Improvement) A methodology for managing continual Improvement by using a Quality Management System. TQM establishes a Culture involving all people in the Organization in a Process of continual monitoring and improvement.
Transaction	A discrete Function performed by an IT Service. For example transferring money from one bank account to another. A single Transaction may involve numerous additions, deletions and modifications of data. Either all of these complete successfully or none of them is carried out.
Transition	(Service Transition) A change in state, corresponding to a movement of an IT Service or other Configuration Item from one Lifecycle status to the next.

Transition Planning and Support	(Service Transition) The Process responsible for Planning all Service Transition Processes and co-coordinating the resources that they require. These Service Transition Processes are Change Management, Service Asset and Configuration Management, Release and Deployment Management, Service Validation and Testing, Evaluation, and Knowledge Management.
Trend Analysis	(Continual Service Improvement) Analysis of data to identify time related patterns. Trend Analysis is used in Problem Management to identify common Failures or fragile Configuration Items, and in Capacity Management as a Modeling tool to predict future behavior. It is also used as a management tool for identifying deficiencies in IT Service Management Processes.
Tuning	The Activity responsible for Planning Changes to make the most efficient use of Resources. Tuning is part of Performance Management, which also includes Performance Monitoring and implementation of the required Changes.
Type I Service Provider	(Service Strategy) An Internal Service Provider that is embedded within a Business Unit. There may be several Type I Service Providers within an Organization.
Type II Service Provider	(Service Strategy) An Internal Service Provider that provides shared IT Services to more than one Business Unit.
Type III Service Provider	(Service Strategy) A Service Provider that provides IT Services to External Customers.
Underpinning Contract (UC)	(Service Design) A Contract between an IT Service Provider and a Third Party. The Third Party provides goods or Services that support delivery of an IT Service to a Customer. The Underpinning Contract defines targets and responsibilities that are required to meet agreed Service Level Targets in an SLA.
Unit Cost	(Service Strategy) The Cost to the IT Service Provider of providing a single Component of an IT Service. For example the Cost of a single desktop PC, or of a single Transaction.
Urgency	(Service Transition) (Service Design) A measure of how long it will be until an Incident, Problem or Change has a significant Impact on the Business. For example a high Impact Incident may have low Urgency, if the Impact will not affect the Business until the end of the financial year. Impact and Urgency are used to assign Priority.
Usability	(Service Design) The ease with which an Application, product, or IT Service can be used. Usability Requirements are often included in a Statement of Requirements.
Use Case	(Service Design) A technique used to define required functionality and Objectives, and to Design Tests. Use Cases define realistic scenarios that describe interactions between Users and an IT Service or other System. See Change Case.
User	A person who uses the IT Service on a day-to-day basis. Users are distinct from Customers, as some Customers do not use the IT Service directly.

User Profile (UP)	(Service Strategy) A pattern of User demand for IT Services. Each User Profile includes one or more Patterns of Business Activity.
Utility	(Service Strategy) Functionality offered by a Product or Service to meet a particular need. Utility is often summarized as "what it does". See Service Utility.
Validation	(Service Transition) An Activity that ensures a new or changed IT Service, Process, Plan, or other Deliverable meets the needs of the Business. Validation ensures that Business Requirements are met even though these may have changed since the original Design. See Verification, Acceptance, Qualification, Service Validation and Testing.
Value Chain	(Service Strategy) A sequence of Processes that creates a product or Service that is of value to a Customer. Each step of the sequence builds on the previous steps and contributes to the overall product or Service. See Value Network.
Value for Money	An informal measure of Cost Effectiveness. Value for Money is often based on a comparison with the Cost of alternatives. See Cost Benefit Analysis.
Value Network	(Service Strategy) A complex set of Relationships between two or more groups or organizations. Value is generated through exchange of knowledge, information, goods or Services. See Value Chain, Partnership.
Value on Investment (VOI)	(Continual Service Improvement) A measurement of the expected benefit of an investment. VOI considers both financial and intangible benefits. See Return on Investment.
Variable Cost	(Service Strategy) A Cost that depends on how much the IT Service is used, how many products are produced, the number and type of Users, or something else that cannot be fixed in advance. See Variable Cost Dynamics.
Variable Cost Dynamics	(Service Strategy) A technique used to understand how overall Costs are impacted by the many complex variable elements that contribute to the provision of IT Services.
Variance	The difference between a planned value and the actual measured value. Commonly used in Financial Management, Capacity Management and Service Level Management, but could apply in any area where Plans are in place.
Verification	(Service Transition) An Activity that ensures a new or changed IT Service, Process, Plan, or other Deliverable is complete, accurate, Reliable and matches its Design Specification. See Validation, Acceptance, Service Validation and Testing.

Verification and Audit	(Service Transition) The Activities responsible for ensuring that information in the CMDB is accurate and that all Configuration Items have been identified and recorded in the CMDB. Verification includes routine checks that are part of other Processes. For example, verifying the serial number of a desktop PC when a User logs an Incident. Audit is a periodic, formal check.
Version	(Service Transition) A Version is used to identify a specific Baseline of a Configuration Item. Versions typically use a naming convention that enables the sequence or date of each Baseline to be identified. For example Payroll Application Version 3 contains updated functionality from Version 2.
Vision	A description of what the Organization intends to become in the future. A Vision is created by senior management and is used to help influence Culture and Strategic Planning.
Vital Business Function (VBF)	(Service Design) A Function of a Business Process which is critical to the success of the Business. Vital Business Functions are an important consideration of Business Continuity Management, IT Service Continuity Management and Availability Management.
Vulnerability	A weakness that could be exploited by a Threat. For example an open firewall port, a password that is never changed, or a flammable carpet. A missing Control is also considered to be a Vulnerability.
Warm Standby	Synonym for Intermediate Recovery.
Warranty	(Service Strategy) A promise or guarantee that a product or Service will meet its agreed Requirements. See Service Validation and Testing, Service Warranty.
Work in Progress (WIP)	A Status that means Activities have started but are not yet complete. It is commonly used as a Status for Incidents, Problems, Changes etc.
Work Instruction	A Document containing detailed instructions that specify exactly what steps to follow to carry out an Activity. A Work Instruction contains much more detail than a Procedure and is only created if very detailed instructions are needed.
Workaround	(Service Operation) Reducing or eliminating the Impact of an Incident or Problem for which a full Resolution is not yet available. For example by restarting a failed Configuration Item. Workarounds for Problems are documented in Known Error Records. Workarounds for Incidents that do not have associated Problem Records are documented in the Incident Record.
Workload	The Resources required to deliver an identifiable part of an IT Service. Workloads may be Categorized by Users, groups of Users, or Functions within the IT Service. This is used to assist in analyzing and managing the Capacity, Performance and Utilization of Configuration Items and IT Services. The term Workload is sometimes used as a synonym for Throughput.

References

Bon, J. van (ed.) (2007). *Foundations of IT Service Management - based on ITIL V3*. Zaltbommel: Van Haren Publishing

Office of Government Commerce (2007). *ITIL: Service Design*. London: The Stationary Office

Office of Government Commerce (2007). *Glossary ITIL Version 3*: http://www.best-management-practice.com

Index

ITIL Books
The Official Books from itSMF

Foundations of IT Service Management Based on ITIL®V3
Now updated to encompass all of the implications of the V3 refresh of ITIL, the new V3 Foundations book looks at Best Practices, focusing on the Lifecycle approach, and covering the ITIL Service Lifecycle, processes and functions for Service Strategy, Service Design, Service Operation, Service Transition and Continual Service Improvement.
ISBN: 978 908753057 0 (ENGLISH EDITION)
PRICE €39.95 EXCL TAX

Foundations of IT Service Management Based on ITIL®
The bestselling ITIL® V2 edition of this popular guide is available as usual, with 13 language options to give you the widest possible global perspective on this important subject.
ISBN: 978 907721258 5 (ENGLISH EDITION)
PRICE €39.95 EXCL TAX

IT Service Management Based on ITIL®V3: A Pocket Guide
A concise summary for ITIL®V3, providing a quick and portable reference tool to this leading set of best practices for IT Service Management.
ISBN: 978 908753102 7 (ENGLISH EDITION)
PRICE €14.95 EXCL TAX

Van Haren Publishing (VHP) is a leading international publisher, specializing in best practice titles for IT management and business management. VHP publishes in 14 languages, and has sales and distribution agents in over 40 countries worldwide: www.vanharen.net

ISO/IEC 20000
The Official Books from itSMF

ISO/IEC 20000: An Introduction
Promoting awareness of the certification for organizations within the IT Service Management environment.
ISBN: 978 908753081 5 (ENGLISH EDITION)
PRICE €49.95 EXCL TAX

Implementing ISO/IEC 20000 Certification: The Roadmap
Practical advice, to assist readers through the requirements of the standard, the scoping, the project approach, the certification procedure and management of the certification.
ISBN: 978 908753082 2
PRICE €39.95 EXCL TAX

ISO/IEC 20000: A Pocket Guide
A quick and accessible guide to the fundamental requirements for corporate certification.
ISBN: 978 907721279 0 (ENGLISH EDITION)
PRICE €14.95 EXCL TAX

Other leading ITSM Books from itSMF

Metrics for IT Service Management

A general guide to the use of metrics as a mechanism to control and steer IT service organizations, with consideration of the design and implementation of metrics in service organizations using industry standard frameworks.

ISBN: 978 907721269 1
PRICE €39.95 EXCL TAX

Six Sigma for IT Management

The first book to provide a coherent view and guidance for using the Six Sigma approach successfully in IT Service Management, whilst aiming to merge both Six Sigma and ITIL® into a single unified approach to continuous improvement. Six Sigma for IT Management: A Pocket Guide is also available.

ISBN: 978 907721230 1 (ENGLISH EDITION)
PRICE €39.95 EXCL TAX

Frameworks for IT Management

An unparalleled guide to the myriad of IT management instruments currently available to IT and business managers. Frameworks for IT Management: A Pocket Guide is also available.

ISBN: 978 907721290 5 (ENGLISH EDITION)
PRICE €39.95 EXCL TAX

IT Governance based on CobiT 4.1: A Management Guide

Detailed information on the overall process model as well as the theory behind it.

ISBN: 978 90 8753116 4 (ENGLISH EDITION)
PRICE €20,75 EXCL TAX

Printed in Great Britain
by Amazon.co.uk, Ltd.,
Marston Gate.